Building a Strategic Plan
for Your Life and Business

Building a Strategic Plan for Your Life and Business

DISCOVER THE SECRET OF THE GREATS

John M. Hawkins

iUniverse, Inc.
Bloomington

Building a Strategic Plan for Your Life and Business
Discover the Secret of the Greats

Copyright © 2013 by John M. Hawkins

All rights reserved. No part of this book may be used or reproduced by any means, graphic, electronic, or mechanical, including photocopying, recording, taping or by any information storage retrieval system without the written permission of the publisher except in the case of brief quotations embodied in critical articles and reviews.

iUniverse books may be ordered through booksellers or by contacting:

iUniverse
1663 Liberty Drive
Bloomington, IN 47403
www.iuniverse.com
1-800-Authors (1-800-288-4677)

Because of the dynamic nature of the Internet, any web addresses or links contained in this book may have changed since publication and may no longer be valid. The views expressed in this work are solely those of the author and do not necessarily reflect the views of the publisher, and the publisher hereby disclaims any responsibility for them.

Any people depicted in stock imagery provided by Thinkstock are models, and such images are being used for illustrative purposes only.

Certain stock imagery © Thinkstock.

ISBN: 978-1-4697-4624-1 (sc)
ISBN: 978-1-4697-4625-8 (e)
ISBN: 978-1-4697-4626-5 (dj)

Printed in the United States of America

iUniverse rev. date: 4/9/2013

Dedication

To my daughters, Emily, Ashley, and Haley. I want you to feel that you own your destiny. Here is a planning tool that I have used to reach my goals. I hope you find it useful in your lives.

Contents

Preface	ix
Introduction	xiii
Success All Around You	1
Strategic Plans	11
Self-Assessment	30
Building Your Life Plan	41
Creating the Plan	62
Strategic Plan by Example	84
Vision	100
Goals	118
Strategies	124
Objectives	135
Initiatives	142
Road Maps	146
Projects	150
Building Your Strategic Plan	153
Living the Strategic Plan	161
Practice the Strategic Plan	172
Conclusion	185
Works Cited	193

Preface

WHEN I WAS A young boy, my father used to tell me stories about the great legends in business. He would talk about all their great accomplishments and the power and wealth they had accumulated. The legends included J. Paul Getty, T. Boone Pickens, Warren Buffett, and others. I felt as though I could sit and listen to the stories of these greats for hours. They had made a difference not only in their own lives, but also in the lives of others. I can recall being fascinated by the stories, but I believed that anyone could achieve greatness if they wanted to. These greats had accomplished what others could not. As a youth, I wondered why others did not achieve such success. In my simple mind, the reason they didn't was because they must not have wanted to.

One of the greats was J. Paul Getty—a man who was able to accumulate a lot of wealth. When Mr. Getty passed, he donated his fortune to the J. Paul Getty Trust. One of the museums run from his trust is in Los Angeles, which has nearly 1.8 million visitors each year. The trust runs on a simple vision: "the diffusion of artistic and general knowledge" (The J. Paul Getty Trust, 2011). It amazes me that an entity can run off a single vision statement; only seven words drive the actions of the entity.

As I got older, I quickly began to realize that it was much harder to be successful than I had originally thought. The greats who found a way to be immensely successful must have had knowledge that the rest of the world did not; they had power that the rest of the world could only admire. The idea of becoming great and accomplishing my dreams became a fading memory; ideas of becoming successful like the greats were boyish thoughts. But I never could completely dismiss the idea that someday I would be successful. I continued searching for the answers to how I should be thinking. I had no mentor, no one to show me how to think differently. Each time I thought of my dreams, I imagined a heavy weight on my shoulders. It affected my mood and my ability to make decisions. I decided that I must wait for the perfect idea, and when that idea came, I would be ready to accomplish my dream.

As I grew from a young boy to a man, I never forgot what my dad taught me about the great ones but was still at a disadvantage; I still did not know how to think like the greats. I did not have the thought process to even comprehend the amazing feats the greats had accomplished.

I wondered:

Did they have a plan to help them become the successes they were?

Did they know more than others? Did someone teach them?

What strategy did they use to become so successful?

As I moved on in my life, I went to work for the greats—not a single man or woman, but the great organizations that are collectively able to do what the great men my father spoke of accomplished. It wasn't until I found my way into the corporate life that I realized that large organizations had found ways to accomplish great things just like the greats. They have found ways to master the economies and produce the products and services that the world depends on. These organizations have the ability to grow and dominate the fields they are in.

It took a while to find the secret, but after getting a glimpse into the strategic-planning process of many great organizations, I realized that I had found what I was looking for. The secret was not a secret at all. Organizations, like the greats, had the ability to make the strategic decisions that led to their success. And they had the ability to continue to make great decisions. They took risks and invested in the strategies that in many cases led to huge dividends. One of the tools the companies used to make the decisions is a strategic plan.

The strategic plan is a planning methodology that forces organizations to think strategically about the vision for the organization. The vision is the ideal of what they want to become. The result of the process is a plan to get them to accomplish those goals. Those who have mastered the secrets of the strategic plan and take the risks have a better chance of getting the results that give them the ability to rise to power in the organization.

Building a Strategic Plan for Your Life and Business explores how to use the components of a strategic plan to help you create and realize the vision of who you want to be. You are going to go through a systematic methodology to help you plan for your future. You are going to learn how to create a strategic plan to help you identify where you want to be in one year—or in five, ten, or twenty. You are going to learn how to align your vision with the strategic plan and come up with a strategy to help you achieve your goals. Not only will the plan help you achieve your goals, but it will also help you define initiatives and projects you can start working on to help you get closer to your goals and realize your vision. This plan that you are going to create is going to get you the success that you have been looking for to get you to the end state you have been dreaming of.

Introduction

THINK ABOUT THE CELEBRITIES and successful people that you know of. Could you sum up some of these great people in only a few words? Donald Trump: real estate mogul. Walt Disney: cartoonist. Oprah Winfrey: talk show host. Before they were great, Oprah, Walt Disney, and Donald Trump were just ordinary people—with just one exception: the paths they were on were very different from the ones of others around them. They were on a path to success—and, unbeknownst to them, success beyond their wildest dreams. Their vision of who they could become was in alignment with their plan, a plan that would lead them to greatness beyond what they could dream of.

These are very successful people who have built billion-dollar businesses and yet are generally known for one thing. You might now know them for more than the single accomplishment, but they started somewhere with a single success. They knew what challenges they should be focusing on and were led by their internal vision of who they wanted to be—the vision that drove their daily activities—and then they had to take a series of steps to help them realize their vision.

For many of us, becoming mega-wealthy is not a realistic vision. However, you can use a similar thought process to improve the quality of your life. You can use the technique to create a plan to meet your vision. You can use the technique to help you get to your goals in five, ten, or twenty years. The greats did it, and if you look around you, you'll see that others are doing it too.

Imagine for a moment that you have been given the power of strategic thinking, just like the greats: you are now able to make strategic decisions. Finding a way to invest in those decisions could pay huge dividends to you. Making the right decisions could better your life and the lives of your family members as well as those who will come to work for you or have their lives bettered by your vision.

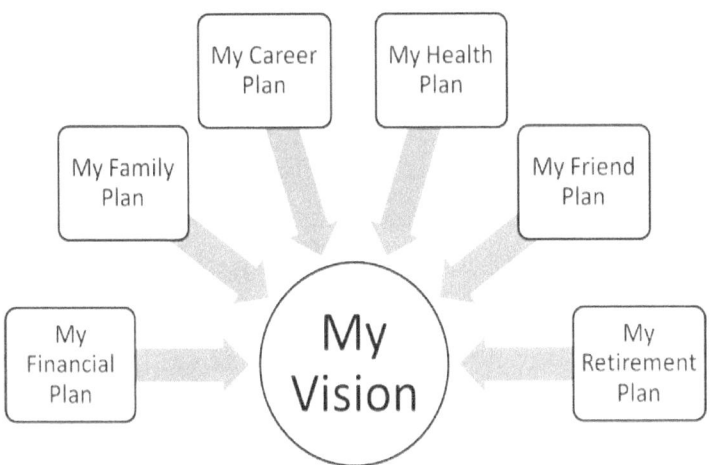

Figure 1 : My Vision

Planning and achieving your vision is not only for those who are mega-wealthy and famous. Think about the people you meet in life who have accomplishments you admire. They might be people who have competed in the Olympics, been a professional athlete, written a book, started a successful business, or maybe just were really great people. The point is that no matter what you are trying to accomplish, there are those who are successful. Before reaching their success they had a vision of what they wanted to accomplish. They might not have fully known what their actions would lead to, but they had the ability to see something in themselves that they grew from a vision into reality.

I truly believe that we all have the ability to realize our dreams. If you have a vision of where you want to be in life, why not go for it? Others around you are realizing their dreams—why not realize your dreams as well? John

Q. Public: orthodontist. Joe Shmoe: retired at age fifty. Jane Doe: philanthropist. Jackie Doe: lives in a paid-off house. What is your vision?

Have you ever been part of a team that was really successful? You might have played on a team in school. Did you do well on a test or close a big deal? Did you have a really successful fund-raiser where you accomplished something no one thought you could? Go back in your mind and think about how you felt when the team pulled through and realized the vision. Imagine if there was a way to have feelings of success all the time.

There are lots of people out there every day who want to be a better person, find a way to climb the corporate ladder, or grow their business to high levels. You might think about what life would be like if you could be that person. What would you do with your time and money if you were able to meet all your goals in life? How would you feel taking your business from its first dollar to selling it to a large corporation for more money than you could ever dream of? The supersuccessful have found out a system that allows them to be successful.

If financial success is not your idea of success, then have you thought what life would be like if you had the ability to make a difference in the lives of others around you? If you could run a nonprofit or had the time you needed to help others less fortunate? You open the newspaper or read an article online about how someone has started a new charity and raised millions of dollars to help a less fortunate group. Do you know someone who is in a position where they were able to meet all their goals and objectives and achieve the success they needed?

What if corporate or charitable success is not your cup of tea? If they are not, what would it feel like to realize your potential as a professional athlete, a dancer, a singer, or a movie star? How would it feel to star in a show all about you? There are people who are able to realize their vision and get the leading roles and make their way to the top of the entertainment ladder. You might look at them and say, *How did they do it*? You might be more talented. Just take a look at shows like *American Idol*. They prove the point that there are performers out there who are better than those who have risen to mega-stardom.

You might be smarter and more talented, and yet they are the ones with the success. What is the secret they have that you do not that has catapulted them to stardom and success? There are people every day who are realizing their dreams and visions. They are living the dream, becoming everything they want to be in life. They have found a way to get to the end state that is making them feel fulfilled as a person. You might look at them and say, *I could do that*, or, *How did a simple idea like they started out with get them to where they are*? They have a secret that they are not going to share with you. They have every opportunity that you have, with the exception of one. They are strategic thinkers; they are people who figured out what was important to spend their time on that would benefit them rather than spending time on nonstrategic initiatives. They have their success by focusing on the key initiatives, whereas you focused on nonstrategic initiatives.

In this book, you are going to learn how to use a methodology to create success, to create the vision of what you want to be in the future. The vision of you in the future could be based on a simple goal that you have for yourself. Later in the process, you can use this technique to create a multidimensional plan to help you realize the complex vision that you have for yourself, a vision that is so complex and multifaceted that you will need help implementing and maintaining all your success. At this point in the journey, you will have others working on your strategic vision and plan rather than you working on other peoples' strategic plans. How you use the framework is up to you. You can choose to go all in or review the methodology and decide that it isn't right for you. You have the control over how much success you want to plan for.

You can determine how much time you want to spend on planning your life vision and goals. You can spend five minutes a day, five minutes a month, or five minutes a year. Your success is all going to be based on how much time you want to commit to the plan. If you become fluent in building strategic plans, you might be able to be successful by making the right decisions rather than making decisions that are going to hinder your progress.

You have the ability to prioritize the plan and determine the amount of time needed to be able to accomplish the goals and vision that have been defined. The quicker you become a strategic thinker, the sooner you will see results. It isn't about how much time you are spending on the vision but more that you develop the skills to make the best decision to get you closer to your goals and ultimate vision.

Realizing your plan is going to take you from your current state through a transitional period that will get you to the future state.

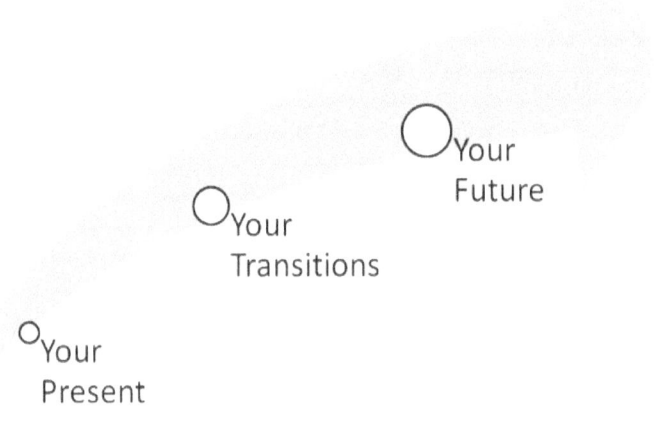

Figure 2 : Present to Future

You are going to need to define what that future-state vision for you should look like. This is going to be from an ideal state, not what you expect things to be like in the future but your ideal vision, what you dream of. You will identify where you are today and create the gaps and the strategic plan to get you to that future state. You will come up with a concrete plan with actionable steps to help you become who you want to be one, five, ten, and twenty years from now. You are going to use the process we define to create your life strategic plan.

Success All Around You

ACHIEVING YOUR GOALS CAN be as simple as being lucky and being in the right place at the right time. Sounds easy to do, right? Get born into the right family, have parents who work hard to get you a job as a child actor, have grandparents who worked hard and built a multimillion-dollar company. It sounds like a simple way to realize your vision and goals, right? Well, that may work for a small portion of the population, but what about the rest of us, who are not able to be reborn into the right family? To reach your goals, you have to be smarter and make the right strategic decisions in life.

We all have visions of who we want to be and how we want our life to play out. At a young age, we are bold and feel that we can do anything we set our minds to. Turn on a TV or drive down the right streets, and you can see success. You see the big houses in the neighborhood and the nice cars; you hear stories about how celebrities and others have unlimited access to resources. Many of these superstars started life as humbly as you did. For reasons known only to them, they found a way to become successful. If you sat down with them and asked them how they did it, I am sure they would not say it was handed to them or that they inherited their lot in life, right?

Many of us live our lives reacting to life and all the hurdles and obstacles that come our way. You become so good at dodging the little challenges in life and are careful not to make too many waves when things are going well. When you take the approach of only reacting to life's hurdles, this isn't necessarily going to help you achieve your vision. By reacting to life, you are not in control of the vision; you are not defining the vision and defining your strategic plan. You are letting your environment, your peers, and the challenges that life throws at you set your vision. By doing this, your chances of achieving the vision you set for yourself dwindle significantly.

At one point in your life, you, like many people, had an idea or plan of what you wanted to do, and maybe some unforeseen event came up and messed up all your plans. Think about what you do for a living. Is the vision you had in college or as a young person the same vision you have today? You planned on going to grad school but just couldn't afford it; you wanted to become an MD but didn't get into medical school. So you settled for something else. Now evaluate where you are today and fast-forward your life ten years.

- Would you be satisfied with your life as it is today?
- Are you making the money that you need to meet your vision and goals?

You might have accomplished a number of goals but still feel the sense of emptiness, that there is more you can do. Even when you accomplish goals, the odds are that soon after the accomplishment you will feel unsatisfied. This goes back to your childhood. Think back to your dreams as a young person; you might have envisioned a romantic and idyllic life. You had plans of doing great and wonderful things that seem out of reach to you now. The news flash is that they are still in reach if you want them. You can still accomplish what you want; you have just become overwhelmed by the harsh realities of life that have hijacked your thinking. When you were young, you thought that life should be enjoyed, and you dreamed of early retirement and a life of success and perhaps fame.

So what changed? Did you forget about the road you wanted to take? Were the challenges of life too difficult? Or did you just not know the right steps to take during your journey? The reason you are not accomplishing your vision is because you are on a strategic plan that is not in alignment with the vision you want. You are on an ad hoc strategic plan that may or may not get you to where you want to go.

Consider the vision you had as a child versus what you have become.

- Is what you are today in alignment with the childhood vision?
- Are you getting what you want out of life?
- If you are not, then what is different? Did you have a happier outcome in mind?
- Did you have a vision with more money or more fame or picture yourself as a better person?
- What did you envision versus what you are getting out of life?

You most likely had the happier scenario. You were full of hope and optimism. As a child, there was no limit to what you could accomplish. In school you had a choice, which could have limited your success. You were told in school that you could achieve anything you wanted. And if you did not do well in school, you sealed your fate to earn less money, live a less happy life, and limit your potential. What the education factory did not take into account was that education is not the only strategic plan you can follow. There are other strategic plans that can get you to your goals. Those around you may have set the ceiling and helped to limit your thinking, but you don't have to let that stand in your way. Your fate is not sealed; you still have the same opportunities to make the right decision, which you didn't the first time. At the time, you could not know any better; at that age you were not a strategic thinker—and all the greats are strategic thinkers.

You were not a strategic thinker because at that age you did not know how to think strategically. You got your information from your parents and from friends, teachers, and others in your circle of influence. The problem with listening to those around you is that if they are not strategic thinkers, then you are not learning how to think strategically. You are making the decisions not based on your vision but on the vision of others, which differs from yours. Always consider the source and filter the information that is being given to you. There could be an ulterior motive behind the information you are getting. A parent or friend could influence your decision to study abroad because they want to be close to you, but studying abroad was something that was in alignment with your vision.

Life Stages

The person you are today is not the same person you will be in six months, twelve months, or ten years. The biggest difference is your age, but there are many other differences. The state you are in today is the current state; these are all the things about you that make up who you are today. Depending on the environment and decisions you make, you will gradually move to the future-state you.

As previously mentioned, the future state can be driven by your vision of who you want to be or you can go through life letting your environment and others dictate your future state.

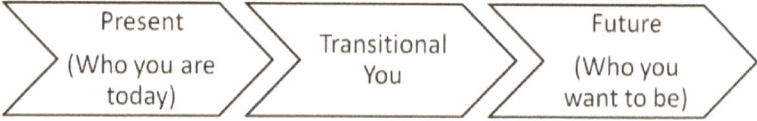

Figure 3 : Life Transitions

Life Timeline

Draw on a piece of paper a line with an arrow going from left to right. Draw on that line your life as you saw it from a teenager or young adult. Put down your school, what you wanted to accomplish in life, who you wanted to help, and even when you planned on retiring. Take a look at the life timeline and think about how you would feel if you were able to accomplish all those things you wrote down. The answer is obviously pretty good, since these are your goals and dreams.

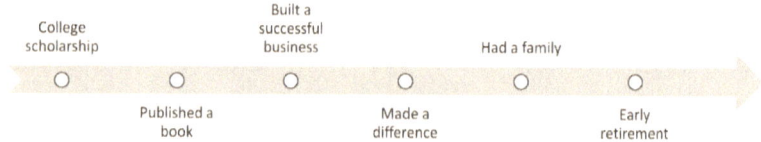

Figure 4 : Ideal Life

Now draw that same arrow from left to right and write on the arrow where you are today.

- Did you not get the scholarships you wanted and are now deep in financial debt?
- Did you finish school but get the wrong degree?
- Did you have a family before getting your career underway?
- Do you need to have two jobs to make ends meet?
- How close are you to your retirement?

Your current state should be pretty eye-opening and, if you are someone who had big aspirations, could be pretty painful. This is your life, what you have accomplished thus far, and you are not where you want to be. You used to have big dreams and ambitions but have not been able to realize them.

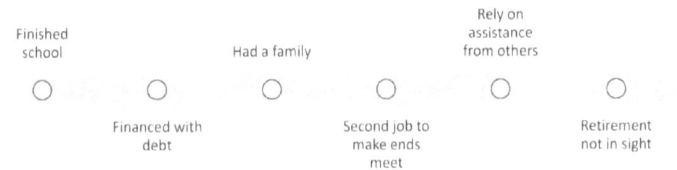

Figure 5 : The Reality

Take a look back at your current-state timeline and determine where you went wrong.

- What decisions did you make that were not strategic?

- Did you make those decisions on your own, or did you have someone help you make the decisions?

Think back to the life you envisioned. Will the steps you are taking *today* get you to that final state? My guess is that some will and others will take you further from the vision. Only you can answer why you are focusing on the steps that lead you away from your goal. Perhaps you don't know how to, or perhaps you feel emotionally attached to what you are doing; only you know the answer. The sad part is that you are smart enough to accomplish the goals, but what you are lacking is the ability to think and execute strategic decisions about your life. To determine what you need to focus on can be difficult; there are so many moving parts to life. You need a framework you can work from to build a formula for your life.

Regardless of who made the decisions, they were wrong. Now focus your attention on the future-state vision of what you want to be; is this a valid future state or future vision for you still? If so, how far off are you from achieving the goals you outlined for yourself? If you want to stop making the wrong decisions, then you have to start thinking strategically from now on.

- Commit to yourself that you are going to be a strategic thinker.

One thing that is constant in life is change. Change can be good or change can be bad. There is a great deal of satisfaction when you accomplish something that has merit and value. Think back to your childhood. What did it feel like learning to tie your shoe? I recall trying many times and failing, but with more practice I became very good at tying my shoes. When I figured out how to repeatedly do it there was a great deal of satisfaction. Think about the little things in life that still give you that satisfaction.

Do you have a talent or skill that others do not? Are you able to wow your friends by being able to curl your tongue or do a cartwheel? Getting a sense of accomplishment is built into the fabric of our beings. We are always looking for the sense of satisfaction from what we do. That same feeling of accomplishment never goes away; we are always looking for that feeling that gives us the satisfaction. The goals may change, but the fundamental high we get never changes.

As you get older, accomplishments you once had as a child become less and less defined. You were told that if you did well in school, you would have great success—or if you learned to hit the golf ball straight, you would be ready for the PGA tour. As you matured, you realized that things might not be as clear-cut as you once thought. There are so many choices to make and paths you could be focusing your time on.

- What path do you choose?

- What choices are going to get you to the goals that have set out in your mind?
- How will you find a way to assess the present, define your future, and build the plan to get there?

Strategic Plans

"SIMPLY PUT, STRATEGIC PLANNING determines where an organization is going over the next year or more, how it's going to get there and how it'll know if it got there or not" (McNamara, 2011). There is more than one single approach to building a plan. "There are a variety of perspectives, models and approaches used in strategic planning" (McNamara, 2011). One of the tenets of this book is to think strategically but act tactically, and we are going to include some of the more tactical elements to the strategic plan. For the purpose of the book, we are going to define the components of the plan as "vision, goals, strategies, objectives, initiatives, road maps, and projects" (Scott, 2009). For our purposes, we will focus on these components to create our life plan. As we mentioned before, there really isn't a pure version of a strategic plan. There are many derivatives, and we chose these attributes from the strategic-planning process. The goal is to get you to think about your planning in a different way. In thinking differently about your planning process, you will build the "secret sauce" you can use over and over again to build your success.

In the plan, we have an attribute called vision. Vision is the idyllic or future state of where we want to be. Vision is a more descriptive way to describe what we are trying to accomplish with our strategic plan. While there is no formalized methodology for building a strategic plan, it is possible to take a systematic approach. The strategic plan includes road maps. We can tie in other strategic plans into a single vision. A strategic plan that links in other strategic plans is multidimensional. The higher-level vision is a sum of the parts, as there are many strategic plans linked together. Figure 6 shows a multilevel strategic plan and demonstrates how you can use the composition of other strategic plans to define your future-state vision.

The strategic plan is a tool, and the end result is a plan we can follow to meet our vision or goal. Like any plan, the strategic plan should have a logical starting point. It should have qualitative and quantitative objectives to define what the success criteria are. We need to know when we are successful and when we are not so successful. The plan must also support the vision we are setting out to achieve. The strategic plan should start out at a high level and progressively move to more and more detail.

To successfully create a strategic plan, you must alter your current-state way of thinking from tactical to strategic. You must become a strategic thinker. Starting work on your strategic plan will force you to organize your thoughts in such a way that details become less of a priority and you will start focusing more on strategic initiatives. The more strategic plans you create, the better you will be at thinking strategically. Creating your strategic plan will take many iterations or tries before you are able to create one that has a realistic vision with goals that are in alignment with the vision. Once you are successful with your strategic plan, you can become the architect of your life.

Figure 6 : Multilevel Strategic Plan

By creating your own strategic plans you are using the tools that the greats are using even as we speak to build the future-state world we will live in. By creating your own strategic plan you will be one of the strategic thinkers who pore over the visions of how the world will operate. To get to that level will take some time, but it is not outside of your reach. The best way to start thinking strategically is to start taking control of the future state of your life. Start with the simple, mundane, day-to-day activities. By creating strategic plans even for mundane visions and goals, you will learn the valuable lesson and over time start to think strategically. Your strategic plans might be simplistic to start with, but over time as you create the vision they will become plans or strategic plans to help you achieve the vision. The vision could be a simple vision such as being healthy, or you might have something more complex like running a successful business.

You can use the strategic plan to test what you do on a daily basis. For example, if I eat junk food every day and do not exercise, are these strategies in alignment with my vision of being at a healthy weight?

The simple answer is no, but until you put it in that context it is hard to rationalize not eating the junk food because it tastes so good. A strategic plan can help with such rationalization.

Can you see yourself being the strategic thinker? Are you able to see beyond the day-to-day and think about the vision and big picture? As you transition into a strategic thinker, you are the one who can drive direction in the world. You can be the one who owns the vision and ultimately the plan to meet the vision. You can be successful just like all the greats. Just look at all the greats in this world: they had a vision of becoming someone or creating something that we never could have imagined. They had the ability to see the future and created a plan to get them to realize the future goal. The architects and strategic thinkers in life are right now architecting your future world. They are designing the cars you will drive, the homes you will live in, the future social media, and the books you will read. They are creating the strategies that you will soon be following.

Start Your Journey

All journeys start with a single step, and you could argue that before the single step there was a lot of planning that needed to take place. Imagine going on a journey without a plan; instead you just take steps. Where will your journey take you? What destinations will you visit along the way? Who could possibly answer these questions, right?

You started a journey without a plan. Life is the same way. You have started on a journey and could be halfway through it and have just been taking steps. How is that any way to live? For many, it might be okay, while others can't live that way. Your strategic plan is going to give you a systematic way to help you accomplish those dreams and desires you have for yourself. Creating any plan at this point is better than not having a plan. You should be in a better position by just thinking about your vision and life even if you never build a strategic plan.

Learning to build the strategic plan is the first step in becoming a strategic thinker. The plan you create will need nurturing and guidance to help meet your vision. You should consider aligning yourself with other strategic thinkers. If you are a visionary and have the problems of the world solved but associate with people who are realists who cannot see the vision, then you are going to have a tough time continuing to be the visionary. Their self-doubt and constant negative comments and sky-is-falling mentality will keep you from being the visionary you want to be. It will only be when you are able to prove that your theories are correct that those tactical thinkers will start to see benefit in your thinking. It might seem like a nonsensical thought, but try it out. Talk strategy to someone who is focused on the present, the here and now, and they will find every reason to discredit your ideas and pass you off as a dreamer.

Behind the science of the strategic plan there is an artistic piece as well that you will need to learn. Thinking strategically is not just about quantitative measures; there are some qualitative aspects behind it. You will need to understand human psychology, understand the history of what has worked and not worked, and be a realist to some degree so that you know what is plausible and what is not. You as the strategic thinker are going to be held responsible for the strategies that work and those that do not work. You will need to figure out over time when to modify the strategies or at some point you might determine that the vision you set up is not really in alignment with who you are. It is important to remain flexible. The result you had in mind might not be the one you achieve but could still be rewarding nonetheless. You as the strategist will also need to develop thick skin. For some odd reason, people take comfort when others are in their same predicament. They will want you to fail so that they can say, "I told you that wouldn't work." Think about the people you know. I am sure you know people who are always right and never try anything new, and when you try something outside of the norm they are the first to say I told you so. Develop thick skin while you are testing and perfecting your strategic-planning skills. You will need it to deal with those who do not think strategically.

A Strategic Plan Is Dynamic

A strategic plan is not a static entity; it will ebb and flow with your life. Unforeseen events happen; births, deaths, the loss of a job, and other events will impact your strategic plan. You must be ready to embrace the new reality and change the plan to meet the new environment. It isn't easy to give up visions, but being successful might come in a form that you did not expect. Your definition of success might be limited by your experiences and judgment. It might be possible to get the same feeling of satisfaction doing something that is not in your current vision but is equally satisfying. When you start to delve into your strategic plan, you might find that there is more than one possible outcome. You can change the ending of the story and it will be even more exciting than you anticipated. The greats all felt like they could do something beyond the norm.

Understanding that strategic plans are not perfect and will need frequent revisiting is important to keep a positive attitude. You will start to second-guess yourself daily as you create your vision, building your confidence in thinking strategically. You will wonder if the vision is even possible. You might try to convince yourself that you do not have the skills to pull this off and that going back to the status quo is the way to go. Before you give up hope on your strategic plan, trust in the process, trust in your abilities, and trust you can accomplish all the great successes that others do on a daily basis. A way to do this is to revisit the strategic plan frequently to ensure that you are in alignment, that the vision is realistic. It is okay to go down a path for five or six years and realize, *Wait, this isn't the right path for me. I need to evaluate my strategic plan; this just doesn't feel right to me.* As you create the vision and put the timeline in place to achieve the objectives, keep a placeholder for revisiting the strategic plan itself. Creating a strategic plan will be a continual process. You might build your strategic plan over time; you might revisit the vision on your birthday or make changes to the strategic plan at the start of the new year.

When you start out building a strategic plan, you will think about it daily, maybe even hourly; it will be like watching the paint dry on a newly painted wall. You will eventually find a balance where you start to trust in the process and can let it go. For the simple strategic plans, you might set a daily reminder to review the progress. If you have a practice strategic plan you might even start to accomplish the vision in one day. In these cases, you won't need the monitoring.

Invest the Time

Strategic plans take time up front. Unlike executing on someone else's strategic plan, the strategic plan will require your up-front attention. You are going to need to put in more work in the beginning than you are used to. It will be a transition for you; something that is outside your comfort zone. The strategy and direction were something that you previously leaned on someone else for. Now you are put in the driver's seat. You are the one who is setting the project plan, the vision, and everything else that is needed to accomplish the vision. You can do this by systematically looking at your strategic plan and setting a cadence where you come back to plan and ask the questions that need to be asked. If you are someone who focuses on the tactical, then you should have no problem envisioning executing the strategy. Give yourself the permission to try this; give yourself the time to get it right and trust in your ability to do it. Ensure that the vision is in alignment with who you are and is realistic, or you will need to adjust.

Strategic Plans Are Subjective

Strategic plans are subjective, and it is difficult to measure performance when you are relying on qualitative information. How can you measure performance on your hopes, dreams, and fears all coming into one place? You are going to have emotions when you think about the successful opportunities you had and did not capitalize on. There might be a sense of anxiety when you look at your strategic plan and accomplishments. Facing where you are can be difficult for just about everyone—not just those who are ultrasuccessful, but everyone. Think about the one-hit wonders who had tons of fame and money and now have nothing. Your experiences and life-changing events can, and will, have an effect on you emotionally. Taking into account the emotional aspect and your desire to be successful, you will still need a way to rationally and logically look for alignment in the strategic plan.

Vision: Is this a vision that I want? Or is this something that someone else has willed on me? In either case, you can choose to accept the vision and build the strategic plan toward success or throw the vision away altogether. It is important to not get wrapped up in who came up with the idea for the vision. If you have a friend who nags and nags you to get into a particular field because you are a natural fit, then it is worth exploring it as a potential vision, even though that was the field your father might have been in and you want nothing to do with it. Try to take the emotion out of it and determine what is in your best interest. If you give up a good opportunity, you had better have an alternate lined up before dismissing the viable one.

Goal: Assuming you have the best vision possible, have weighed the alternatives, and have validated that this is the vision for you, you will now need to create the goals to support that vision. Ask yourself if the goals are in alignment with the vision. Try to visualize that you have accomplished all the goals.

- If you accomplished the defined goals, would you realize the vision?
- The goals meet the vision, but are they realistic, and can you achieve them in your lifetime?

The goals to support the vision are a piece of the vision. Ensuring alignment with the goals and vision is, for all intents and purposes, a piece of the vision. The sum of the part equals the whole.

Strategies: An important question to consider while building and executing on the strategic plan is whether the strategies are working. Not every strategy is a good one, and if it is a good strategy, it might not work in every situation. You might need to demonstrate some leadership and make an executive decision to change your strategies from time to time if they are not working. You can also have a strategy that you thought might help get you to an end state but found that it just wasn't in alignment with the goals or that the strategy was taking too long to realize any benefits. And you may have determined that there is a better or faster way to accomplish what you are trying to do. Keep your strategies fresh. They are what will help you realize the goals and what you will need to be able to do well to accomplish the vision. It is also worthwhile to mention that you don't have to come up with all the strategies yourself; rely on the insight of others. You don't have to give them your whole strategic plan and say, "What do you think?" Just give them pieces of it. You could say, "I am thinking about auditioning for *American Idol*. What do you think my chances are?" Then belt out a rendition of your favorite song.

Objectives: Up to this point in the plan, you have been working at a pretty high level. The objectives are the tangible milestones you need to meet to accomplish the goals you have set forth. Foremost, you can look to see if you need to check for the alignment of objectives to goals. With proper alignment, just ask yourself what milestones you have hit since you started the strategic plan. If you have been on the strategic plan for a year and have not accomplished any milestones, then there is a problem.

Your objectives and milestones are a good benchmark to see if your strategies are working. If you are not meeting milestones, then your initiatives are not effective, or your strategy could be incorrect. Check for alignment with the strategies and do a reality check. *Are my goals something that I can achieve? What am I not doing or doing that keeps me from accomplishing them?*

Initiatives: You will next need to accomplish your clearly defined objectives. The initiatives are broad actions that you will be doing to meet the objectives. As with all the other attributes, check for alignment: Did I define the right initiatives? Are they too complicated? Am I so constrained by time that I just have not had a chance to look at them? Do I need to free up time on my calendar to focus on these initiatives? Your initiatives are what you will be doing to accomplish the objectives defined by the strategies. These are the tactical day-to-day activities.

Road Maps (Time-Sequenced Initiatives): Including your road maps in your strategic plan is a way to start to incorporate your finalized strategic plans and other road maps into your vision. Let's say you have a vision to start a business. You started simply enough by creating the business, getting your first customers, and selling your products and services. Now that you have a successful business, there is going to be a lot more to manage, and you might also need to delegate the activities and planning within the business. It might be that you need to have a single strategic plan for the business and perhaps a marketing and operations strategic plan to support the business. Determining when you need to expand the strategic plan is entirely up to you. Do so when the complexity of the strategic plan increases or if you have multiple leaders who are responsible for strategy. You can encapsulate the plans into road maps and incorporate them into your overall plan.

Projects: Projects are activities that organize initiatives to meet the objectives. If you have a number of related initiatives that need to be met, it makes sense to group them together into a single project. The projects are what you are going to execute. The projects are the most tactical you are going to get in the strategic-planning process. This is where you go for it. All the planning is done, and you are in alignment with the vision. Just execute the strategy and attain the vision. At the project level, you should be in alignment with your strategic plan.

Cadence

Your strategic plan is not going to maintain itself. It is not something that you can set up and just let run. There should be checkpoints with the strategic plan to check on your progress. The cadence is the regular visits to the strategic plan to check for alignment. The cadence is when you check on the project status to see if you are achieving the objectives and getting closer to the goal. You have the ability to determine how often you check in on your strategic plan. Your cadence is just as important as the strategic plan itself. Without you attending to the strategic plan, you reduce the chances of success.

Getting a cadence in place to visit and revisit the strategic plan helps the strategic plan take on a life of its own. It can become a living entity that you can refer to. When you are feeling down and want a pick-me-up, you can get out the strategic plan and see the progress you have made, or if you are looking for a little motivation you can see that you are behind on your progress and get the kick you need. Your strategic plans are all about you and your visions. There is never a bad time to review the strategic plan.

In creating your cadence, there are some things you should be thinking about. You should always have the vision in mind. This is the reason you are creating the strategic plan in the first place. If you did not have a vision, then the strategic plan would be a moot point. If you need to adjust the vision, then you need to validate that the rest of the attributes are all still in alignment with the new vision and then validate what you have accomplished. If you have not accomplished what you expected, then why have you not? There must be a reason for not meeting the objectives *you* laid out. Identify what is not working and adjust accordingly; as life changes, you should be adding and removing the initiatives not in alignment with the vision from the plan. You then should measure the success, always taking into account how effective you are at executing the strategic plan.

It is easy to create a vision and say that you want to achieve a result and then push it off until next year. Measuring your success or lack thereof should give you the encouragement you need to either ramp up the effort or change the plan to meet your vision. And finally, be realistic. Many people will underestimate how long it will take them to accomplish their goals. It is better to be a realist and set the expectations according to your capabilities than to push so hard that you lose interest or give up. Get yourself in the habit of going through the strategic-plan life cycle to make sure the strategic plan is the best plan to meet your vision.

In life, there is a life cycle we are all on; you are affected by an environmental change and are forced to adapt. This change is all part of the life-cycle process. This happens in our family, our life, our job, etc. To account for that in your plan, you need to make decisions that are going to impact the plan. Being able to adapt means that you never know which problems you are going to need to solve. If all the problems you had to solve were similar to prior ones, life would be easy.

Your experiences, which take time to build, are what you will rely on for making those decisions. There is a way to cheat the experience. If you can find the right resource with the experience, you can leverage their experience to be able to make an informed decision. Given you are relying on others, you will need to always consider the source and get advice from those you see as being successful.

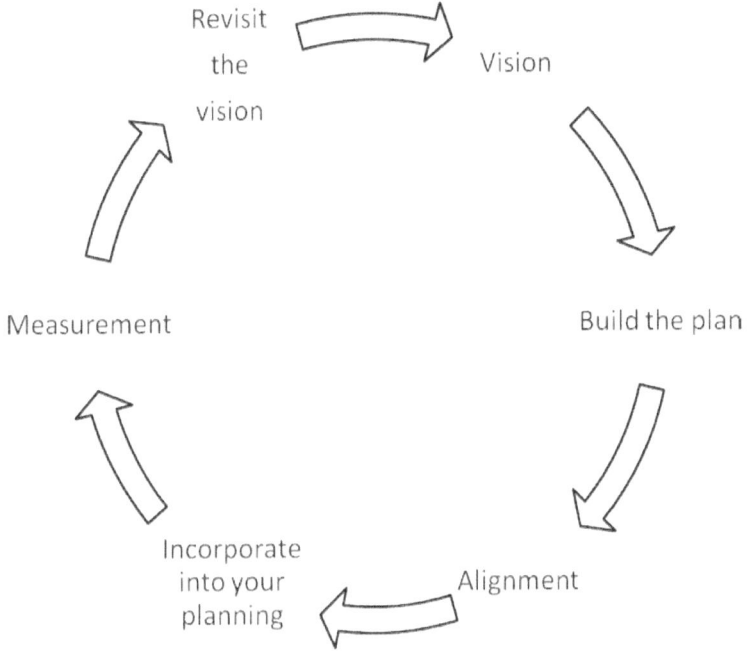

Figure 7 : My Strategic-Plan Life Cycle

Once you finalize a strategy or an action that you need to take, you are going to need to take some time testing it and adopting the way of looking at things through the perspective of a strategic plan. Think back to the little accomplishments you were able to make as a young child, such as learning to tie your shoes. At the time, you might have been frustrated and felt like you would never, ever achieve that goal. But you did. You tied your shoes, and now you can repeatedly tie shoes every day. Creating your strategic plan is going to feel uncomfortable at first, but over time it will feel more and more natural.

Predict Your Future State

When defining your vision, when you think about your life and where you want to be, is it clear in your mind? Most likely not, but think about the past. I am sure that in most cases it is clearer than the future vision. You know where you came from; most everyone has a clear understanding of where they came from. If you choose not to change a thing, just advance the clock five years—that is where you will be in five years' time. You will need to answer if you like that place or not—are you satisfied with the accomplishments you have had thus far?

Do you feel that you have achieved all the success you want?

Just as you have a clear view of where you came from, there are people who can clearly see the steps they take and how they are going to get them to a future state.

The future state of your life will look just like where you are today if you don't change a thing; what you are today will be the vision or future state.

You were good at thinking about your future state as a child in school. School is predictable: you know that you are going to move from preschool to kindergarten to grade school to middle school, etc. Try closing your eyes and thinking about yourself and where you will be in five years. If in the future you are in the same place you are today, will that be acceptable to you?

- Do you like the person you are?
- Are you healthy and fit?
- Are you at a healthy weight, happily married, making all the money you want in life?

If you are, then that is wonderful. Make no changes to your life; the future-state you is what you will become. If, on the other hand, you open your eyes and feel a sense of anxiety from the exercise, you might need to work on your vision.

SELF-ASSESSMENT

EVERYONE IS NOT CREATED equal, right? How many times in life do you need to be told that life isn't fair? We are constantly repeating the question in our minds. You might have missed out on a promotion you thought you were qualified for or lost a job when someone less capable was kept. Your children might not seem as smart as your neighbor's children, or you may have suffered some other inequity.

The truth about you is that you might be more capable than others in some areas and less capable in other areas. As a strategic thinker, you will need to have an honest self-assessment about who you are. You are the person who needs to understand what your strengths and weaknesses are. With a good understanding of what you are good at and not good at, you should look for opportunities that you are qualified to pursue.

SWOT

A tool used in business is the SWOT analysis. SWOT stands for strengths, weaknesses, opportunities, and threats. SWOT is a commonly used business tool with some "contradictory views on the Origin" (Friesner, 2011). Regardless of origin, we can take the tool and apply it to our lives. The tool is broken up into four quadrants. The upper left is strengths: What are you good at? The right quadrant covers weaknesses: What you are not so good at and should avoid. The bottom left quadrant concerns your opportunities. Each of us has different opportunities in life; what ones are open to you? And finally in the lower right corner are the threats.

The SWOT analysis tool can be used to help you get a snapshot of your current state. Your current state is who you are today and includes both the internal factors (the internal you) and external factors (your environment). The figure on the next page shows the tool and how you can internalize it to meet your needs.

Building a Strategic Plan for Your Life and Business

Figure 8 : SWOT Tool

My Strengths

So what exactly are your strengths? Can you readily list them? Your strengths can be both qualitative and quantitative. Strengths are something that differentiates you from others, in a good way. Your strengths are unique to you and only you. You might share some individual strengths with others, but the combination is all you. Your strengths are assets to you when you are in a challenging situation. If you are in a PE class and are challenged to run a mile and you have a strength in running, you are going to have the advantage. If you are a faster runner than others, you are going to be successful at accomplishing the task at hand.

Think about all the challenges you have had over your life, where there were some challenges that just seemed right up your alley—challenges that might seem daunting to others but to you were exciting. People might look at you funny and say that you are completely crazy. But you are not; the challenge that was put in front of you suited a strength of yours. Think about this: If you are an introvert and like to meticulously work on things and have a few close friends but are not generally social, how are you going to feel when you are dropped into a highly social environment? You are most likely going to feel rather uncomfortable. If your goal is to be successful, how will you get that feeling of success when you are put into situations that continually make you feel uncomfortable? You have two choices: you can either grow in a way you did not expect or you can focus more on the activities that you do feel comfortable with. It is hard to say if the experience will help you grow in a good way or in a bad way; you just need to be able to identify what are your strengths, and those strengths become visible when you are faced with a challenge.

- I am a people person.
- I love to talk.
- I am good at solving problems.

- I am a fast runner.
- I am a good listener.
- I accomplish my goals.

What are some of your strengths?

Weaknesses

Many of us have no problem identifying our weaknesses. You might be able to quickly rattle off your weaknesses without giving it much thought. You can determine your weaknesses in the same way you determine your strengths. When you are facing a challenging situation, how do you feel? Imagine that you are driving down the street and your car just stops running. You take your car to the mechanic and get a quote to repair it. He informs you that the car would cost more than it is worth to fix. How do you react to this? Are you excited about getting a new car and don't think about anything else? Do you start shopping right away? Or do you shut down because you are so put off by the thought of negotiating with the dealer? Your first reactions to challenging situations can be a leading indicator of your weaknesses.

You might gather from your car-buying experience that your weakness is in negotiating but you have a strength in doing research and finding the best deal. There might be some folks out there who are just excited by the opportunity to wheel and deal; they get a lot of satisfaction out of negotiating with the salesman. A weakness for you does not mean it will always be a weakness; it may be something that you can turn into a strength.

Weaknesses:

- I am not a good speaker.
- I am afraid of people.
- I am not good at sports.
- I am a pessimist.
- I have trouble building relationships.

What are some of your weaknesses?

Opportunities

Opportunities are all around you, or at least that is what you have been told—yet you are having trouble finding them. So the key to opportunities is that they are mostly going to be external to you. You do not find opportunities in your living room or by sequestering yourself in your vacation home. Your opportunities are all going to be external. This means that you will need to go out and find them. They are not going to come to you.

Given that your opportunities are all external, you must expose yourself to the outside world to determine them. There are countless ways to do this. Getting yourself out into the world means that you must be engaging with other human beings to determine what is an opportunity. You can do this a number of ways. You can socialize with groups who share interests. You can read the newspaper, Internet blogs, and articles. You can talk to your neighbor while doing yard work. You never know when an opportunity will come along. But you must find a way to identify what is an opportunity and what is not.

School is a great example of giving you opportunities. You are in an environment where you spend eight hours a day with like-minded individuals. Going to school is a requirement, so you will have exposure to the superintelligent, the musically gifted, and the athletes. By engaging in conversations with those around you, you may find an opportunity that will set you up for life. You might find that you like sports and get involved with a sport that is suited toward one of your strengths and then go on to a successful life in that field.

Opportunities are all around you. They are external, which means that you need to find a way to interact with the outside world so that you can find the opportunities that are suited to your strengths and pursue them. You must also identify any weakness that is keeping you from being social and find a way to interact with the outside world. If you do not identify those weaknesses that keep you from social events, you will never be put in a position to get opportunity, and you must have the opportunity to realize your success.

Opportunities come in a number of ways.

- Your parent owns a business, so you have an opportunity to learn about business.
- You are enrolled at an Ivy League school.
- A family friend is starting a business.
- There is an opportunity for a promotion at work.

There are always opportunities out there; you just need to be aware of them. And something we will not cover but that is equally important is that you must be prepared to take advantage of the opportunity. By focusing on those opportunities that are in alignment with your strengths, you will have a better opportunity for taking advantage of them.

Threats

Threats are external to you but can threaten your ability to capitalize on opportunities. You should identify what is a threat to you and find a way to navigate around it. For example, if an opportunity came up for a promotion in your department and there are other candidates who have a strength in that area, those other candidates are threats to your taking advantage of that opportunity.

Threats, like opportunities, are only realized in the outside world. This means that to find a threat you first need to identify an opportunity that you want to capitalize on. The threats can come from business, family, and just about anything you can think of. If you are dating someone who has a superfriendly coworker who takes an interest in your date, then that coworker is a threat. If you have children and they are in a social situation with children who are drug users, then the drug-using friends are a threat.

The key to handling threats is to assess if this is a threat that you are prepared to tackle and if you have a strength you can use to mitigate the threat. You might deem that a threat will be so difficult to overcome that you stay away from opportunities that would threaten you. You might as well focus on what you are good at, meaning that it is one of your strengths and that you can overcome the threats and realize the opportunities.

Some threats include

- competition that is better, faster, smarter;
- a better-qualified applicant for a job;
- pressure from your peer group; and
- people with negative comments.

What are some of your threats?

Summary

The SWOT tool is just one the tools you can use to help you do a self-assessment. You can use the strengths, weaknesses, opportunities, and threats to give you a good idea of what you need to work on to help you be better equipped to start the process of self-improvement. The process of self-improvement is to identify and foster your strengths. Identify any covert weaknesses that are keeping you from capitalizing on opportunities. Put yourself in a position to identify opportunities that have threats that can be mitigated by your strengths.

Figure 9 : Goal of SWOT

To become good at strategic planning and capitalizing on your vision, you need to have a good sense of who you are and what your strengths are. The SWOT analysis is a tool that you can use to do your self-assessment. The SWOT tool is not something that is used one time and you are done. It is something that you can use time and time again to foster continual improvement. As you convert weakness to strengths, you want to update the analysis, and as you identify new opportunities, you will also need to update your analysis, as threats come and go with each opportunity. The tool is dynamic and something that will change with your life.

As you read through this book, you should keep in mind your strengths, weaknesses, opportunities, and threats. This is your present or current state, and when you understand what your core competencies are, you stand a better chance of creating a realistic vision for yourself.

Building Your Life Plan

NO TWO PEOPLE ARE the same. Face it—people are different. They think about problems and the subsequent solutions differently. Some folks are glass half-empty, while others are glass half-full. Assuming there are different ways to think, you are going to need to assess the tendencies of your thinking and consciously adjust them. Half-empty or half-full is just a way to show how we can think differently.

For argument's sake, you could also say that there are those who think strategically and those who do not. Are you the big-picture thinker, or do you focus on the day-to-day tasks? The big-picture thinker is someone who thinks at the macro level and focuses on tasks at the micro level. To be successful at planning and executing your vision, you need to be able to identify which problems need strategic thinking and which need tactical thinking and to apply the right thought process to the problem.

Building a strategic plan requires you to think both strategically and tactically. If you are not a strategic thinker, you will need to learn how to think strategically. You may not have heard this before or are being exposed to this for the first time, so what does it mean? It means that you have the ability to think about the big picture and you know the course-grained steps you need to take to get there. You know what accomplishments you need to make to realize your vision. Many nonstrategic thinkers are focused mostly on the tactical. The tactical is the day-to-day activities you are doing that support the big-picture vision. So your vision is to go from being a tactical thinker to being a big-picture thinker.

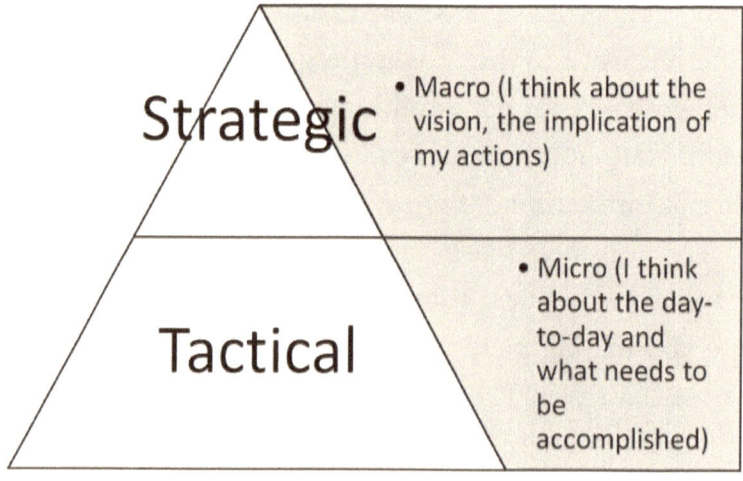

Figure 10 : Strategic Versus Tactical Thinker

Building your strategic plan will take time; understand that your transformation will not happen overnight. Your progress in being able to becoming a great strategic thinker is all up to you. And becoming that great strategic thinker doesn't mean that you just stop doing the tactical. You will just have a better understanding of how the tactical impacts the big picture. The key to beginning to think strategically is to understand how the tactical affects your vision on a day-to-day basis.

You should be starting to have a good understanding of which activities are important in life and which are supporting functions. Given that you are at an early stage in your strategic-planning abilities, you are not only going to have to think strategically but be able to execute tactically as well—that is, until you are so successful that you can start hiring people to do the important tactical things for you.

As mentioned, a strategic plan is really a plan. By now you should realize that you are already following a strategic plan. Granted, it might not be the one you intended to follow or in alignment with the vision you have for yourself. You need to decide if you want to go along with the one that is defined by the happenstances in life rather than the one you envisioned. You might not have a strategic plan in place to meet the objectives, but there are others with plans in place who are moving along their timeline to their vision.

Let's say you have a vision of retiring early, so one of your goals is to retire before age sixty-five.

- Have you solidified your retirement plans?

- Are you in a position where you can meet your goals?

If you are just overcoming obstacles in life, then you are most likely not going to meet the retirement goal. If you have planned adequately for your retirement goal, do you know what it will take to reach that goal early if needed?

Say you have a goal of starting a business. Is working for someone else going to get you closer to that goal? If your goal is to start a business, then what are you waiting for? Are you looking to inherit a business?

Doing the same thing over and over again will not get you any closer to your goals and vision.

You may have a goal of making a difference. Are your actions getting you any closer to that goal? If you are making a difference, is the impact as large as you expected? Can you measure the difference that you are making in the world? If you are falling short, then something needs to change to get you to accomplish the goals to meet the future vision of who you will become.

These are all questions that a strategic thinker would be working on. You need to start thinking strategically about where you are in your current state and how your actions are impacting your future vision. To be a strategic thinker, you need to change how you view life and your decisions; you have to start thinking strategically and start making strategic decisions that are going to benefit you in your life. If you were raised in an environment of strategic thinkers, you will have the upper hand; if not, you have some work do to. You can start becoming that strategic thinker by applying the strategic-planning methodology to everyday decisions.

Everyone has had a certain degree of success in life. To realize that successful life, career, and team, you needed to think about the vision and the goals you needed to accomplish to be successful. Was the vision something that you created? Or was the vision something that the team determined? Regardless of whose idea it was, somehow the team was able to pull together to realize the vision.

The vision should be something that is realistic for the person or team to accomplish. We all have different skills and talents. If you took five musicians and put them in a room and told them they had to write a software accounting program, how successful do you think they would be? They might be able to accomplish the goal, but do they want to? How long would it take to get them retooled to meet the goal?

The definition of success varies from person to person, and to truly feel successful in all you do, you need to have an alignment with your core being. The vision you have of success in life should, to some extent, represent who you are and what you are passionate about. Being successful with something you are passionate about is going to come much easier than something you have little to no interest in, even if you are really good at doing it.

Success Is the Sum of the Parts

Your success isn't just about one great successful moment. Typically, you have to spend time preparing for the opportunity to be successful. If you are part of a team, you most likely practiced together before going out and playing in a big game. You scrimmaged together to understand how to work together as a team. The same is true of the vision you are trying to accomplish. Your vision is going to be made up of a number of smaller successes. You might be able to achieve some smaller successes, but the lasting success will be built of many smaller achievements. Think about the successes you have had in your life; did they take preparation? Or did you just get an opportunity and you did it? Most likely you had a series of events happen in your life to prepare you to be successful when the opportunity presented itself.

It is more important to learn how to be successful than to have success. Think about this for a minute. You see folks who have their fifteen minutes of fame. There are only handfuls who are able to take the fifteen minutes of fame and turn that into something more. They are strategic thinkers, or people who got a job working for a start-up that whet public interest and cashed in. They then moved on to the next start-up and did the same thing. They, too, are strategic thinkers. Are you someone who has put yourself in position to be successful and take advantage of it? Or are you someone who lucked into the opportunity but could not do it again?

Figure 11 : Success-to-Vision Relationship

By thinking differently about accomplishing your goals and visions, you can program your mind for success. No longer will you think about not being able to achieve your objectives, but you will start to look at all long-term visions and start to craft a plan.

When you change how you approach solving challenges, over time you will start thinking differently about solving the challenges. You will start thinking about which goals are worth solving and which are not, and by focusing on the worthwhile goals you will get closer to realizing your vision.

To get to this new way of thinking, you will want to start applying the new thought process on small problems. Yes, problems that seem trivial are seemingly not strategic. You are doing this to give you practice at thinking strategically. Thinking strategically is something that you should be doing on a daily basis. If you don't, when the time comes to make a strategic decision, you will not have had any practice. This practice will also give you confidence in making strategic decisions.

Creating a strategic plan for everyday initiatives might seem unrealistic and daunting. You are creating the plan to practice the skills; you should only have to do the strategic planning until you are proficient and able to focus your time on initiatives that are getting you close to your vision. The idea is that when you have reached a certain level of comfort with the strategic plan, you can reduce the tactical initiatives or pay or entice someone else to work on your initiatives.

The accumulation of a large number of smaller challenges solved will lead you to the success you are looking to achieve. Think critically and logically about how you can achieve your wildest dreams. Think of the success many companies share. These organizations amass billions and billions of dollars by working together toward a common vision. You can apply those same concepts to your life. If a corporate entity is able build a strategic plan to define their vision, then why can't you or I? Why not the small business that aspires to be great?

The strategic-plan thinking is not limited to an age. You could be five years old and start thinking in terms of a strategic plan, with, of course, some help, or in the sunset of your life and still have goals you need to achieve. The only boundaries set are the ones you set. You can build strategic plans as simple or as complex as you want.

Beyond Self-Doubt

When it comes to thinking about success, many people doubt their ability. They have been groomed by society, a family member, their boss, or a team member with self-doubt. "I was never any good at sports, so I don't know if I could accomplish great things." Or "I never really did well in school, so I don't think I could ever achieve my vision." Society, school, or your parents might have groomed you to not think strategically, and you should consider the source; those who influenced you got a similar upbringing. But once you get to a certain age you are using those people as a crutch, as an excuse for not being successful.

Unsolicited Advice

Watch out for people with unsolicited advice. Many people have a problem controlling what they say. You know the people who do this in your life. You mention something you are interested in doing, and because it doesn't interest them or they have some secondhand information, they feel empowered to give you unsolicited advice. The best thing you can do is ignore what they say; for every person like that who has a comment, you can find another with an opposing view.

Follow your passion, do what you are good at, and take what others say with a grain of salt. You are always going to run into people with unsolicited advice. You are on the right course, and you know yourself better than anyone.

You know you can accomplish your vision; you know you can do this. You, too, can think strategically and achieve greatness. The only limiting factor is you. You are the one who has to change your daily thinking from a tactical thinker to a strategic one. You are the one who needs to start writing down the visions you have; you are the one who needs to have the discipline to start thinking like a winner. If you decide you cannot do it or do not have the discipline or the will, then choose not to and be done. If you think you can do it, then you can—get beyond the self-doubt and try it.

How Do I Start?

Creating your strategic plan starts out very simply. You start at a high level, keeping detail to a minimum. The more detail you put in the vision, the better chance you have of getting sidetracked with details, talking yourself out of the vision, or losing track of the overall vision. As you progress through steps in the strategic plan, you will start to add detail that will give you a plan to get you to that end state. By the end of the process, you will have a detailed execution plan to help you get to realize your end state—the state that you desire, that you dream of in the quiet moments of the evening when you think about all you can be but are not yet.

Define the Scope

- What am I looking to solve?
- Is this a tactical strategic plan I am creating to solve a specific problem?
- Is this a strategic plan that defines what I want to accomplish in life?
- What is the scope of the vision?

Start with tactical plans. A tactical strategic plan might start with a vision like "I am a good friend," "I am a great tennis player," "I can speed-read a novel in two hours." These are more tactical visions, which you can solve with a strategic-planning methodology.

You could also create plans around more complex visions like "I solved world hunger" or "My children are good people" or "I am respected in the community." As you can see, a smaller-scope strategic plan with fewer dependencies is going to be easier to realize than a multidimensional strategic plan with multiple touch points.

Once you have your scope defined, you can create the vision statement for that strategic plan. Start with a simple problem with a limited scope so that you can gain confidence in the process and do not have to wait a long period of time to know if you are successful or not.

I Can't Do It

Being successful in life is not easy; it requires will, vision, preparation, and opportunity to give you a chance to accomplish the goals you have set out before you. To accomplish your vision you need to put aside the self-doubt and focus on the positive "I can do it" attitude.

When talking about successful people with those who are not, you might get negative comments like they were successful because they had things handed to them or they were born with good looks or had parents who helped them get successful. Or maybe they had more opportunities in their lives that gave them the ability to achieve their visions. Yes, they may have come into money or had a family business handed to them. But that isn't real success; they are the custodians of the success that a family member bestowed upon them. What you are witnessing is the strategic thinking of their parents. They are benefiting not because of what they have been given but due to the lessons learned from their parents. Just because you were not born into money or a well-connected family does not mean that you have limited potential. It does mean that you are going to have to work harder to find mentors who can help you think strategically.

Start Sooner Rather Than Later

If you have a great idea or vision and no one has tried to solve the problem you are solving, then time is of the essence. I have seen many gifted visionaries share ideas, blueprints, and drawings of some really neat stuff before the product or service was ever on the market. They complain that they had the ideas before someone else who got it to market faster, cheaper, or better. They had the vision but lacked the skills needed to build the strategic plan to accomplish that vision. The idea is of no value, and if you do not have the steps required to accomplish it you will not be successful. When you think about someone who has been successful, he also may have experienced many of the doubts you are feeling. He found a way to deal with the pressure and think strategically through the problem, to create a strategic plan for success and accomplish the vision.

There are physical limitations in life, but when it comes to mental ones you are in control and have the ability to solve any problem you choose to. There is one limitation: *time*. So choose the problems carefully—yes, you can solve all problems in time, but do you have enough time to solve them in?

Think Small

You have a great vision of where you want to be; you

envision you are a leader in your area of focus or have just won a major sporting event. It is important for you to keep those visions of greatness on the back burner while you develop your strategic-plan skills.

Have you ever heard that practice makes perfect? Well, it doesn't; perfect practice makes perfect. Start applying strategic-planning skills to everyday events for which you know the outcome. Having in mind an expected outcome will allow you to start to think strategically about even the smallest of accomplishments. Keep in mind that it is most important to learn how to think. Start thinking about being successful, and analyze the successful decisions that others are making. If you can get yourself into a mode of being successful with little things, you can apply that methodology to the bigger things in life.

What Is Success?

You might have heard the phrase "Success breeds success." Think about it; the phrase is open to interpretation. The success is not just reserved for those with a lot of success but for those with little successes as well. Personalize the statement so that you can take some ownership of your success. The phrase might have meaning, but when you take it and own the statement, you have empowered yourself. It is a statement you can use to live your life by.

- "[My] success breeds [my] success."
- "My little successes breed big success."

The difference between those who are megasuccessful and those who are not is that they had a strategic plan that led to success. They enjoyed the little successes that kept them moving on to bigger and bigger ones until one day they had the success that you long to have—more success than you can handle.

Changing How You Think

Whether you like it or not, we are all following a strategic plan that will lead us to our final destination. You have to ask yourself, *Do I like where my strategic plan is taking me?* If the answer is yes, then do nothing. But if the activities you are engaged in are not in alignment with where you want to go, then consider modifying your strategic plan. You can have input in your strategic plan or take the strategic plan as it comes along, taking the good with the bad and dealing with the hurdles one at a time. You might be happy with this approach, taking life as it comes, taking the good with the bad, going with the flow. And this is perfectly okay; not everyone has the need to create a vision of what she wants to be or become. For many, though, it is not okay to just sit around and let things happen.

Successful people have also been following strategic plans. Whether they call them strategic plans or not, they are successful. They found a way to think strategically. They took input from their surroundings and environment and might have consulted an expert and have created a system to make them successful. They took that success and expanded on it with more and more successes.

Think about their power and how powerful you would feel if you could make the strategic decisions of those who are supersuccessful and use that thinking to act tactically and become successful in your own right.

Today your vision might not be as grandiose as some and you might not have the skills to maintain success in your current state. Think about that. If you got a business handed down to you, would you know what to do? There are a lot of headaches involved with owning your own business. But if you could become a strategic thinker, you would be better prepared to think strategically about your vision and about accomplishing the goals that would be in reach. And you would have similar feelings to those people who are successful have. Thinking strategically works for lots of people; just look around at those who have found success. Think about your life and all you want to accomplish. Now think about all you have accomplished to date. What are all the large and small success milestones you have had in your life? Looking back on those successes, how good would it feel to be the person who accomplished those milestones?

- What would it feel like if you could have similar feelings of success on a daily basis?
- What would it feel like to have the ability to retire early or have money each year for exotic

vacations, learn to paint, play golf, or reach any other life goal you have in mind?

What Do I Need to Change?

Achieving your vision is within reach. Others are successful, so why not you? You are not successful because you are not thinking like a successful person. As a result, you are helping others to realize their visions rather than your own. Successful people have the ability to think strategically about their lives, have a vision of where they want to go, and spend their time on the things that are going to get them there. They then convince others to implement the vision either through the goodness of their hearts or through payment in the form of a job.

Ask yourself, *If I had the information that those who have accomplished great success have, would I not be able to follow in their footsteps?*

Would that not increase your chance for success?

Think about it. If you have the step-by-step plan that told you all you had to do to be successful, would you do it?

If you could take all the wisdom of the successful thinkers and start to think strategically about your life and had a way to effect change, how would your life change?

Old Habits Die Hard

Changing any habit takes a lot of time and effort. Many times it is so hard to keep the new way of doing things that we fall back into the old; it is so much easier to keep the old habits. You might start to rationalize why you should keep those patterns; after all, they have gotten you this far in life. You might think, *If I change what is working I might be more successful, but I could also be less successful.* It is important to think of this as a test drive of the new method. To transition overnight to a new way of thinking is difficult for anyone. Start with a simple "use case," something that is easy to measure in which you can make incremental changes. You don't have to change your whole life, but pick and choose the areas you want to focus on. Our goal is to understand how to think, try the new method, and apply it in small amounts.

Train and Then Trust

A great coach of mine always told me that you have to train and then trust. As you start your transformation to a strategic thinker, you are going to need to train your mind to realize when you need to think strategically and when it is time to think tactically. We do this all the time during life. You sit down to pay your monthly bills. With the stack of bills you might be a master at dividing up the money and putting it into the right piles. You have found ways to get triple value on all your coupons. Yet you still find that your savings is not where it should be.

The tactical thinker can master the couponing and balance the budget.

The strategic thinker might allocate all the monies for the bills and sit back and say, "Well, I don't have enough. What do I need to do?"

- Do I need to bring more money in, or are there ways I can cut back on my expenses?
- If I continue at the current rate, where will I be in one year, two years, five years, etc.?

The strategic thinker understands the big picture and can adjust the strategy accordingly. If this is not you, then your deficit is thinking strategically.

You will need to have both strategic and tactical thinkers to achieve the results—the strategic thinker can look ahead and foresee what the future holds and the tactical ensures that plans are put in place and executed. Your success depends on your ability to think strategically about where you want to go and also have the ability to execute it. The successful person has the ability to think strategically and build systems in place to support those plans.

Successful people are those who understand, from a strategic perspective, the consequences of their actions and thoughts. They have a gut feeling about what is important to accomplish. They have ideas about what is important and take the necessary tactical steps to accomplish their dreams.

Tactical thinkers are great at the details; they are able to accomplish the tactical tasks needed to get the job done. They do not have input on the vision or strategy but are excellent at completing the tasks at hand.

You need to start thinking more strategically. You can use your tactical thinking to solve your strategic issues. As you start to develop your strategic plan, you will need to switch roles between the strategic thinking and the tactical. It will take both skills to build the strategic plan. It will take your ability to determine what tactical activities you are working on and map them to a strategic vision.

Strategic Thinking by Example

Let's say you have a vision that you want to retire early. A logical next thought is that you are going to need a lot of money. For the sake of the argument, say that you determine that you need a million dollars to get there. If you fall into this category you are not a strategic thinker—you have failed the first step. The million dollars is too tactical. Before you can put a dollar value on retirement, you need to define your vision of retirement. If you just jump to a solution, you are not thinking strategically. You are guessing at what you need or repeating rhetoric you have heard from others. Yes, you might be able to retire with that amount of money, but does it meet your vision of retirement? The truth is that you probably don't know—a million dollars sounds like a lot of money. A strategic thinker would say I want to retire early; the second thought is what my life will be like when I am retired. Will I be able to travel? Will I have multiple homes? The strategic thinker is able to piece the vision together in his mind. He has the goal of retirement but also can describe both qualitatively and quantitatively the attributes of the vision.

When you think of your longer-term goals or objectives in life, are you able to see the detail? Or is the picture blurry without a clear definition? As you progress from being a tactical thinker to a visionary one, you should start to see what the future will look like in detail.

CREATING THE PLAN

A STRATEGIC PLAN, FOR all intents and purposes, is a plan designed to help you meet a vision. Once you have defined the plan, you then follow the steps in the strategic plan to get you closer to realizing the vision. A strategic plan can also be applied to short-term initiatives or long-term initiatives; you will typically see them applied to the long term. In this case you will want to apply the concepts of strategic planning to your short-term decisions to get in the habit or practice of thinking strategically.

A strategic plan is typically used in a macro way to accomplish strategic vision, but you can use the principles of the strategic plan for any vision. Consider that you have a family; the family might have a family strategic plan, but so might each of the children in the family. All of the smaller strategic plans contribute to the ultimate vision.

Think about someone you admire for accomplishing his or her vision. Did he or she have a plan for how he or she would accomplish the vision?

Take Oprah Winfrey. Do you think she had a plan in her mind regarding how she would become the success that she is? My guess is that she had a desire to be successful and had a plan that she followed. The planning doesn't just stop with one success; she has to continually work on her vision to continue the success. Whether in the form of a strategic plan or not, somewhere there is a strategy behind all she does.

Consider the decisions you make on a daily basis and their impact on your life. These daily decisions have a direct correlation to what you will become. Not making a decision is making a decision to do nothing. By not making strategic decisions and going with the flow, you are indirectly deciding the fate of who you will become. Think about the things you do on a daily basis; better yet, write down the tasks you accomplish. With a list in hand of all the tasks you do, how many of them are things you want to do versus have to do? How many of them are things that are going to help you make more money or be a better athlete or get you to the retirement goal you are thinking of? When you analyze where the time is being spent, you will most likely find that you are spending more time doing the day-to-day living. The day-to-day living is not going to help you realize the vision you have for yourself.

Doing what others tell you to do or expect you to do will ultimately help them realize their vision, but not your own. I am not saying to not do anything for others, but if you have the type of personality where goals and achieving a vision are important to you, then you must admit it and take the time to get you there. The way to do this is to think strategically about your life and what you are doing and how those daily activities are going to get you to your end goal or vision of what you want to be.

If you could make the same decisions that successful people did, would that not give you a better chance at being successful?

Imagine the possibilities that would open up for you if you could start to think strategically about your life and the goals and dreams you want to accomplish. The difference between those who are successful and those who are not is that they have a way of thinking that allows them to see the results of their actions. They have the ability to focus on what is important in their lives to get them to the vision they see. The greats wanted wealth, to be in control of their own destiny; they want freedom to do as they chose. They were successful at building great empires. The great empires did not build themselves, and after they created these empires, they needed a plan that held them together. The difference is that they had a vision of where they wanted to be and with that vision clear in their mind they chose to make strategic decisions and then acted tactically. The successes they earned fueled more success; it increased their drive to continue their success.

Have you even wondered why those who have made multimillions of dollars on a movie or career continue to work? They could retire; they could do whatever they choose. The reason they don't is that they enjoy the success, they feel good about accomplishments, and they want to feel that way every day.

Sample Strategic Plan

After the holidays, and come January 1, you decide that it is time to change that body image. You take a look at yourself in the mirror and find something that you just do not like and want to change. You open the magazines, newspapers, and online advertisements and see people with the body you wish you could have. So the question is how did they come to be able to maintain their weight when you are not able to? The reason is simple—they have a vision of what they want to look like and they have a strategic plan to help them achieve that vision. If you could take the strategic plan from those in the magazine and apply it to your life, would you not also look fabulous?

The Current Way of Thinking

You look in the mirror and say "I am *fat!*" and then promptly go on about your business. You might also sign up at the gym and eat a couple of healthy meals. That thinking is not good enough; there is no plan. You need a better solution to help meet your goals than to state the obvious and start a course of actions before you have even defined the vision. Consider taking a look at your weight-loss challenge through strategic lenses; define the vision, goals, strategies, objectives, initiatives, road maps, and projects.

Strategic Way of Thinking

- **Vision:**
    - I am healthy. I look and feel great.
- **Goals:**
    - I have low blood pressure.
    - My cholesterol is low.
    - My body mass index (BMI) is in line for my age.
    - I feel great.
- **Strategies:**
    - Join a gym.
    - Count calories.
    - Choose healthy foods.
    - Walk or bike when possible.
- **Objectives:**
    - Lose 1 lb. per week until I meet my goal.
    - Have cholesterol level of less than 200.
    - Work out three times a week.
    - Eat dinners that are half-green.
- **Initiatives:**
    - Exercising can help me lose weight.
    - Eating better will help me feel better.

- **Road maps:**
    - Follow a three-month exercise program recommended by a personal trainer.
    - Follow a three-month nutrition program recommended by a nutritionist.
- **Projects:**
    - Research and join a gym with an exercise program.
    - Meet with my doctor regularly and review my plans; implement a nutrition program.
    - Revamp my wardrobe with exercise gear.

If you create and follow the weight-loss strategic plan, your chances of successfully meeting the goal are much greater than they are with your current way of thinking. The current way is to look in the mirror and say, "I am fat." The strategic-plan way is to come up with a plan to meet the vision of the person you want to become. Think about the two ways of approaching your weight challenges.

Which one makes you feel like there is a reasonable plan to get you to your vision or goal of being a healthy person? You defined a vision of who you want to be and then created the strategic plan to help you get there. Certainly calling yourself fat reflects that you have a low self-esteem, and feeling bad about the condition you have found yourself in, calling yourself fat, might for a brief moment give you the permission you feel you need to continue to be fat. How many people do you think go from being fat to healthy and in shape with an attitude like that? You would think very few, whereas those with the plan who have a solid vision of what they can look like are more likely to meet that goal. The strategic plan, as applied to weight loss, can be applied to all your life visions. You will see in life that those who are able to accomplish their visions have a positive rather than a negative outlook.

Family Strategic Plan

You can also apply the principles of strategic planning to your family life. Think about your family. What are the thoughts that come to mind? Is your family fun? Boring? Do you enjoy the time you spend with them? Now what is the vision you have for your family life? Is the vision different from the reality? Think about how the interactions would be in the vision. You have the power to imagine the future state any way you want. Do you envision family gatherings once a month, with board games and great conversation?

Using the strategic-plan principles, you can define the vision for your family life and create a strategic plan to get you to that vision. To help you get an idea of how not to think, stop for a moment and listen to statements people make about their families, and then take the statements and analyze them. You will probably see that the majority of people are not talking strategically. They are generally focused on the present and not the future. You might hear a lot of comments from nonstrategic thinkers like the following:

- "My family is boring."
- "My family never does anything fun."
- "We never go on a vacation."

These statements all describe the current state for the family. Yes, these may be true statements, but how will this type of thinking help change the future state of the family? The short answer is that it does not and never will. If the vision for the family is "the boring family who never goes on vacation and never has fun," then their statements are in alignment with their vision. The words and actions are in alignment. They might be happy with the way things are, but if you have a vision of being "the happy family who has lots of fun together on family trips," then the statements are not in alignment and you should start thinking strategically about how to change the family dynamics. Consider the strategic way of thinking.

If you were a strategic thinker, you would have an alternative way of thinking about your family. You don't have to accept the current state and can effect change by thinking strategically.

The Strategic Way
- **Vision:**

- I enjoy time with my family.
- **Goals:**
  - When my family is together, we laugh a lot.
  - I can share anything with my family and they support me.
  - Blood is thicker than water.
- **Strategies:**
  - Have meals together.
  - Play games together.
  - Vacation together.
- **Objectives:**
  - Have sit-down meal weekly with family.
  - Write a handwritten note monthly.
  - Spend ten minutes a day talking to each immediate family member.
- **Initiatives:**
  - Schedule fun vacations.
  - Set a dinner time.
  - Calendar entry for each family member's ten minutes.
- **Road maps (time-sequenced initiatives):**
  - Take bowling lessons.
  - Take a cooking class together as a family.
- **Projects:**
  - Set up cooking class; plan meal times suited for all family members.

- Create a vacation budget, plan for first vacation, and take vacation,

Compare the two solutions for the Family Fun Strategic Plan. The one that will most likely yield the best results and get you to the vision of "I enjoy time with my family" is the strategic plan. You might say that my family does not like games or that we have tried all that and it didn't work. As with life and business, not all strategies are going to be successful.

You must try other strategies until you find something that is going to get you closer to your goal and works. If you are still not able to get the desired results, consider that it may take more effort than you had anticipated. At that point, you need to see if the vision is worth the effort you will need to invest to get you the outcome you are looking for.

Small-Business Strategic Plan

In strategic planning for business, consider that you have a small business and you are interested in increasing the sales of that business. If you maintain the status quo, what are the odds that you will realize your vision? You might get lucky and ride an economic wave or have a patent or other competitive advantage. Then you are set, but if you don't have the competitive advantages, then keeping the status quo will most likely not get the benefit you want of increased sales.

So what is the course of action you are going to take to build sales for that business?

If you had a marketing department and deep pockets, you would be able to grow the business on your own. You could hire the right people to help you come up with strategic plan to meet your objective of increasing the sales. There is always a finite amount of time and resources to focus on the things we want to do. What if you had the ability to start thinking strategically, and that strategic thinking gave you the same benefits of hiring that large marketing firm or benefit from hiring a consulting firm?

You can become the strategic thinker by building a strategic plan for your business and working through the strategy until you have come up with a strategic plan.

The Current Way of Thinking
- I am more like an employee for my business.
- I wish I could grow my business.
- At least when I was an employee I had health benefits.
- I hope the economy picks up this year so I can increase my sales.
- I hope my competitor goes out of business, and then I can take over their sales.

The current way of thinking is not going to get you to realize the vision you have of increasing sales. You have done a good job of stating the obvious, but that isn't thinking strategically. You give yourself every excuse in the book for continuing your way of thinking. Consider a different approach; consider a strategic approach by using the principles of the strategic plan.

The Strategic Way

- **Vision:**
    - I've increased my sales this year.
- **Goals:**
    - Many customers are repeat business.
    - Sales margins are increasing.
    - Volume of sales is on the rise.
- **Strategies:**
    - Create a marketing plan.
    - Create strategic alliances with other businesses.
    - Research businesses similar to mine.
    - Increase the perspective of my business with a good online presence.
- **Objectives:**
    - Compare month-to-month sales data.
    - Track sales of alliances.
    - Track sales based on product, price, and promotion.
    - Track each customer's buying habits, and offer special deals based on their purchase behavior.

- **Initiatives:**
  - Start discussions with my repeat customers.
  - Become a trusted adviser to my customers.
  - Find strategic alliance partners.
- **Road maps:**
  - Work with a marketing firm on campaigns.
- **Projects:**
  - Start a database of my customers' names, phone numbers, and e-mail addresses.
  - Increase the web presence of my business.
  - Start monthly newsletter to be e-mailed to my customers.

Think about the two solutions above. The first describes the current state and what you don't like about it. The strategic-plan approach gives you a way to organize your thoughts in a way such that you can logically think through your decisions. You can hope and wish that your business will pick up, but if you do not think strategically and have a defined vision, your odds of achieving that vision decrease with each passing day. The strategic plan gives you a systematic way to start thinking about the vision you are trying to achieve. Keep in mind that a strategic thinker has developed her skills over years and years of trial and error. You may be successful on the first try, but odds are that you will not be. Keep a positive attitude and give yourself goals so that you can be successful to give you confidence and encouragement.

Strategic Plans for Everyday Life

Strategic plans can be applied to every facet of your life; you can apply them to simple things, such as setting up a bank account or deciding what college courses to take. In fact, the simpler the "use case" you have to test the theory on, the more practice you will get in creating strategic plans. The more practice you have working through strategic thinking, the better you will become at it, and if you adopt the concepts and apply them to your decisions, you will become more and more likely to start to realize the vision that you have.

Your daily decisions all have an impact on your life: the road you take to work, the food you eat, the car you drive, the watch you wear, the clothes you wear, the way your body looks. The key is to know which ones are going to have an impact on your future-state vision of yourself and focus on those.

Do you need to create a strategic plan for every little thing in life to be able to achieve your visions? The simple answer is no. Over time, you should be able to internalize the strategic-planning process and you will be able to work through the strategic plan mentally and start acting on your initiatives and objectives. While you are learning the skills, it does help to take notes and write down what you are thinking. If you have your goals written down and stored some place, it makes it that much easier to go back and see if you have achieved them. The best test is to see if you are accomplishing your goals or not. If you are able to accomplish your goals, then there is no need to write them down. If you are not, then you should consider writing the strategic plans. You are still at a stage where you allow your mind to wander.

Trust the Process

As you go through the strategic-plan process, you will need to keep an open mind. You need to trust in the process and trust in yourself and your vision. You know deep down inside what you are capable of. Think about all the areas in your life where you came to a crossroads and needed to make a strategic decision. Think about the series of decisions you had to make just to get where you are today.

- Were you successful in your plan or not?

You have been following a strategic plan up to this point whether you realize it or not. Your thoughts and actions to date, down to the execution, could be codified into a strategic plan. You have the ability to affect your destiny; you can intercept the strategic plan and define a new vision for yourself. The process is deceptively simple, and internalizing the methodology can help you to accomplish the vision you have set out for yourself.

Introduction to Strategic Plans

You have seen the attributes of the strategic plan, but it is time to start exploring them in more detail. As previously stated, there is no set standard for a strategic plan; some of the attributes in a successful strategic plan are vision, goals, strategies, objectives, initiatives, road maps, and projects. These are all pieces you can use to build a strategic plan. The strategic-plan attributes are not set in stone, and you can change these attributes. You will use the ones that make sense to you and perhaps add others and come up with a framework that meets your needs.

This framework is what we are going to use from now until we have internalized the concept of thinking strategically. Once we start to see the successes, the framework will be used less and less frequently with the daily tasks and become more complex with the longer term. As with our strategic plans, the framework has some flexibility to meet the changing times and new ideas. You do not need every one of the attributes, but in a complex strategic plan, you will use all the attributes. These are the areas that you will need to think about when creating your strategic plans. We will cover the key areas in more detail later.

The strategic plan should be high level and can be as complex as you like or as multifaceted as you like. The caveat is that the more complex it is, the more effort it takes to maintain. The strategic plan for our purpose is a means to an end, not the end. We want to use the framework to help us make the best decision to help us realize our vision. Keep that in mind as you are building your strategic plans.

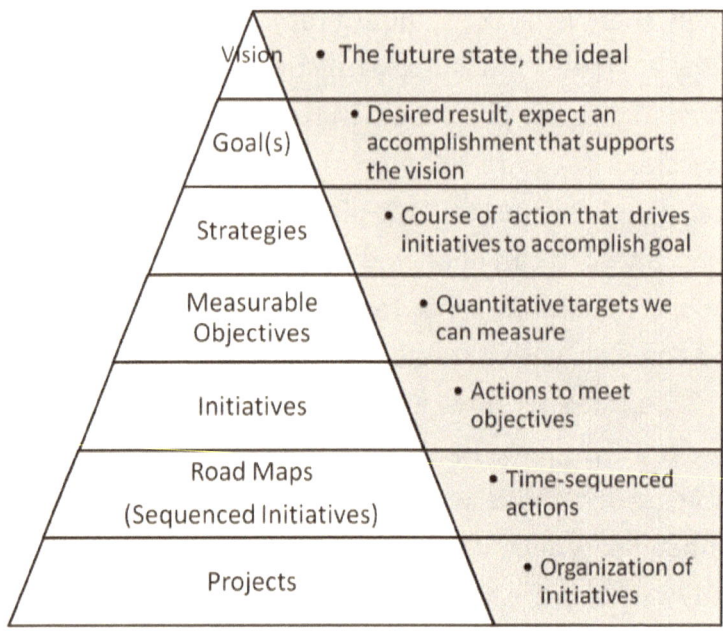

Figure 12 : Some Attributes of a Strategic Plan

To illustrate the strategic-plan capabilities, we are going to go through a sample: "My Friend Strategic Plan." Let's say the vision you have for yourself is to have friends. Taking this use case, you will need to define the vision, goal, strategies, objectives, initiatives, road maps, and projects.

First, we are going to define the vision. The vision is an ideal future state, the pie in the sky. The vision should reflect how you want things to be, not as they are today. So the idyllic vision would be *I have a lot of friends*. The vision does not include details about how we are going to have a lot of friends but that we see ourselves having a lot of friends. The vision should be the ideal; when you think about the vision it should be something you feel you can attain.

Second, with a well-defined vision we now will want to be able to describe the vision in more detail. We know we want to have friends, but that doesn't tell us much. The goals support the vision "to have a lot of friends." We need to set a goal that will help us better define the vision we have set forth. The goal should describe qualitatively the vision of having a lot of friends. To qualify the vision a little more we can define the goal as *build meaningful friendships and be a great friend*. We are looking for not just friends but meaningful friendship and also to be a great friend to others. The goals are that second level of detail; a vision is composed of accomplishing 1–n number of goals, meaning one to any number of goals.

Third, we want to figure out how we can go about meeting the goals we have defined. So ask yourself what ways or strategies you can use to go about meeting the goals. There are so many ways to accomplish the goal, but we cannot do all of them. There simply isn't enough time, so what are some of the strategies you can do to support the goal? You can make friends by meeting new people, or you can rekindle lost friendships. To be a great friend, we need to show that we are interested in those friends. We can do this by keeping a list of all our friends and reaching out to them periodically. The strategies are courses of actions we can take to meet the goals that support the vision.

Fourth, we are now at a point in the strategic-planning process where we want to define the quantitative objectives we want to accomplish. These objectives should all support the strategies we have defined. Now is the time to get specific with what we want to do. An objective could be *I want to have two good friends in six months' time,* or *I want to reconnect with one old friend a month; I want to meet two new people a month.*

Fifth, we identify the initiatives that will help support the objectives we have laid out. You want to think of the things you can do on a consistent basis to support the objectives. An initiative could be to *keep track of my friends;* do you keep in touch with their whereabouts? You could plan to *send out holiday cards, keep track of the people I meet—their names, addresses, and birthdays.* To meet new folks you could have an initiative to *meet people with similar interests,* and when you meet them *give a warm handshake or hug when appropriate.* Initiatives are the broad brush strokes that we can use to meet the objectives. What are the things we can be doing on a daily, weekly, and monthly basis to support the objectives, which support the goal to support the vision?

Sixth, as you build your Friend Strategic Plan there might be other road maps you want to include in the plan or time-line events that you can tie into this strategic plan.

What are the calendars or recurring events I need to be thinking about? It can be as simple as setting up a *monthly birthday-check reminder*. Put a calendar entry to c*heck each month for friends' birthdays, set up yearly holiday mailing,* and perhaps set up *weekly time to focus on friends*. If you are looking for a significant other, you might even sign up for a friend-finder website.

Seventh, what are the projects that you need to have to support the vision? What do you need to have in place to support the vision? You will most likely need to *create a database of my friends in an easy print format*. You might need to *choose a calendaring system to set up my reminders*. Let's say you have not been keeping up to date on your hygiene and that is a reason you have not gotten a lot of friends. So you start a project to *update my wardrobe, get a haircut, and see the dentist*. Also, set up projects to help organize the initiatives you have set forth. You could have a project to create a Facebook page or create business cards to hand out with your information.

My Friend Strategic Plan

When we take all the data, we can create the Friend Strategic Plan.
- **Vision**:
    - I have a lot of friends.
- **Goals**:
    - Build meaningful friendships.
    - Be a great friend.

- **Strategies:**
  - Meet new people and explore friendships.
  - Rekindle lost friendships online and through family.
  - Maintain a list of friends and e-mail or mail updates to them.
  - Meet people with similar interests.
- **Objectives:**
  - Reach out to my friends often.
  - Have lunch with one of my friends or group of friends once a month.
  - Join social groups with people of similar interests.
- **Initiatives:**
  - Send out holiday cards.
  - Keep track of the people I meet; track their names, addresses, and birthdays.
  - Give a warm handshake or hug when appropriate to those I meet.
  - Remember names.
- **Road maps:**
  - Set up monthly birthday-check reminder. Check each month for friends' birthdays.
  - Set up yearly holiday mailing.
- **Projects:**
  - Create a database of my friends in an easy print format; the database will include their first names, last names, e-mail addresses,

dates of birth (DOB), and a comment section.
- Choose a calendaring system to set up my reminders.

Your strategic plan can be simple and fit on a single sheet of paper. You do not need to include all the attributes, but that all depends on what the vision is that you are trying to accomplish. Also keep in mind that life is complicated; keep your strategic plan simple enough to follow. We are also trying to learn the process of how to create strategic plans. When you create your first strategic plan, it might be on target or completely wrong. Investing some time in the process is helpful, but we also want to be able to develop the process so that we can best meet our needs. The strategic plan needed a strategic thinker to see the vision of "I have a lot of friends." To execute the vision, you need to put the tactical thinking in place to meet that vision.

This is your vision and your strategic plan. You are empowered to revisit your vision daily, weekly, monthly, or yearly. As life changes your priorities, your vision can change. In some cases, the vision may not be achievable due to physical or other limitations. Be realistic about the vision and visit your strategic plan often and make updates as needed.

STRATEGIC PLAN BY EXAMPLE

YOU CAN CREATE A strategic plan for your life, for your career, or even for your love life. We want to start thinking about things in a strategic nature and then move to more tactical. If you start out at the tactical level, there are so many details that you will lose focus of what you are trying to accomplish.

Here is a strategic plan around having a house that is paid for. So the vision is to live in a paid-for house.

Vision:

- I live in a house that is paid for.

Not much detail here; we do have questions that need to be answered around the vision. We need to understand more about the vision, "I live in a house that is paid for." What are the details around this vision?

Add some more color to the vision by creating the goals that make it up.

Goal for vision "I live in a house that is paid for":

- I own the home.
- I have more financial flexibility.

Defining the goal of having more financial flexibility gives us a better view of what the vision of paying off the house is like. We still do not know how we are going to accomplish these goals, but it gives us a better understanding of what we are trying to accomplish. And by having a clear vision of what we need to do, we can envision a way to accomplish it.

Dig a little deeper into the plan and define the strategies needed to support the goals.

Strategies: We have a goal, and now we want to come up with a way to meet that goal. There are many ways to go about doing that. You could inherit lots of money, you could win the lottery, you could steal the money, or you could get it in many other ways. The assumption is that you are looking for an ethical strategy, right? I suppose you could use planning for anything, but in this case we are going to focus on ethical means of realizing this vision.

For the sake of the example, let's assume that the strategy of paying down the principal is chosen.

- Make a monthly principal payment to my mortgage in addition to my payment.

- Rent out rooms in my house for cash.
- Use my house as a business.

Objectives: Now you have identified the vision of living in a paid-off home and defined what the goals are, such as you own your home, and you have come up with strategies to do so. Now you need to start thinking about when you want to do this by; the objectives are the qualitative and quantitative benefits you are looking to get from the goals. So in this case, you want to be free and clear in fifteen years or less.

- Pay off home in fifteen years or less.
- If I pay $243 more per month, I can pay my home off in fifteen years. (I have a 100k mortgage over thirty years with a 6 percent interest rate; I pay $596 a month, and $839 per month would pay off the home in fifteen years.)

Initiatives: So you have an objective that you want to pay off the home in fifteen years. Time is ticking; as of today, you have fourteen years and 364 days to accomplish your goal. The initiatives are the broad strokes you need to take to get you to the goal. Applying extra money to the principal will help; you could work extra hours and apply that money to the principal. There are lots of initiatives you could do to help accomplish the objectives.

- Find ways to apply the extra $243 per month to my principal.
- Increase revenues to make principal payments.
- Set up a recurring principal payment in addition to my mortgage.
- Rent out a room in my house.

Road maps: For this strategic plan we are not going to link in other strategic plans at this point. Having a vision of living in a paid-off house is a fairly tactical vision. The more tactical, the less complex you want to make the strategic plan.

- Not applicable (n/a) for this vision.

Projects: You now have all the pieces you need to accomplish your vision of living in your home, free and clear. You defined that you want to live in a paid-off home, that you are going to own the home, and that the home should be paid off in fifteen years. You are going to look into saving money and possibly taking a part-time job. You just need to start organizing everything into projects and start accomplishing the vision. In projects, you will want to take the initiatives and group them as follows:

- Start interviewing potential roommates.

- Work with a financial planner to see where I can cut costs.
- Increase my income, either through a new job or asking for a raise.

Here is the full strategic plan.

- **Vision:**
  - I live in a house that is paid for.
- **Goals:**
  - I own the home.
  - I have more financial flexibility.
- **Strategies:**
  - Make a monthly principal payment to my mortgage in addition to my payment.
- **Objectives:**
  - Pay off home in fifteen years or less.
- **Initiatives:**
  - Find ways to apply the extra $243 per month to my principal.
  - Increase revenues to make additional principal payments.
  - Set up recurring principal payments in addition to my mortgage.
  - Rent out a room in my house.
- **Road maps:**
  - Not applicable (n/a) for this vision.
- **Projects:**
  - Start interviewing potential roommates.

- Work with a financial planner to see where I can cut costs.
- Increase my income, either through a new job or by asking for a raise.

The example strategic plan is fairly simple, but as you can see, now we have a way to go about solving the vision of having the house paid off in fifteen years rather than thirty. These strategic plans can be applied to virtually everything you do in life.

Strategic Plan for Friends

The strategic plans can be used to solve personal goals as well. Think about the vision we defined above: "I have a lot of friends."

Ralph Waldo Emerson wrote, "The only reward of virtue is virtue; the only way to have a friend is to be a friend."

The only way have a friend is to be a friend. Think about it. If you are committed to the above strategic plan, over time you would stand a better chance of meeting your vision rather than the status quo of the current state. By creating a simple Friend Strategic Plan, you will give yourself a plan to realize the vision of having a lot of friends.

Explore how you can increase your friends through a strategic plan.

Vision: We will start with the vision. Perhaps you don't have a lot of friends, so your vision is that you have a lot of friends. We don't know much about the friends. They could be good examples to use or cause us to do things we will regret later. But at this point it doesn't matter—we just want a lot of friends.

I have a lot of friends.

Goal: "I have a lot of friends" doesn't say much about the friendships you have. You should think about the types of friends you want to have. Do you want friends to chat with? Friends to do things with? Friends who have a truck you can borrow? You want to qualify the vision with some goals to better describe your vision.

- Build meaningful friendships with lots of people.
- Have friendships with like-minded people.
- My friends look out for my best interest.

Strategies: With your vision clearly defined, start thinking about the goal; where you find your new friends could make a difference. If you are looking for friends who share your interests and you are a NASCAR enthusiast, you might not find success in looking for friends at a knitting convention. You might, but there might be better strategies to get to your goals. In defining your strategies you want to check for alignment, so a strategy could be to meet new friends and to seek out your past friendships and rekindle them.

- Meet new people and explore friendships.
- Rekindle lost friendships online and through family.
- Join social groups with people of similar interests.

Objectives: The objectives of your Friend Strategic Plan are going to help you know when and if you are successful. What are the milestones you want to reach? You might want to have a good friend in a year's time. The objectives defined for your friends should be qualitative or quantitative enough so that you can determine if and when you are able to reach them. The objectives are how we know that we are making progress toward our goal.

- Reach out to all my friends on a monthly basis, through phone, e-mail, or social media.
- Find a NASCAR enthusiast with whom I can go to races.
- Have lunch with one of my friends or group of friends once a month.
- Greet people daily with a firm handshake and a smile.

Initiatives: The initiatives for your friends will be the broad actions that are going to get you to meet your objectives. So think about the broad actions you could do to get to your goal. The action of keeping track of your friends supports the goals. You could send out holiday cards to your friends. You might also go to events where there are a lot of like-minded people. There are lots of actions you can do to support the strategies and goals you define to help get the friends you are looking for.

- Keep track of my friends.
- Send out holiday cards.
- Keep track of the people I meet; track their names, addresses, and birthdays.
- Go to events that interest me; start talking to people.

Road maps: Road maps will support the strategy. These are the time-sequenced initiatives we have created that tie into our Friend Strategic Plan.

- Set up monthly birthday reminders. Check each month for friends' birthdays.
- Send holiday mail every year.
- Make time to focus on friends each week.

Projects: The projects are the activities that organize initiatives to meet the objectives you have defined. You wanted to find a way to keep track of your friends, so perhaps creating a database of friends would be helpful. You also might come up with an e-mail or mailing list.

The projects are how you want to include the initiatives to meet your vision.

- Create a database of my friends in an easy print format. The database will include their first names, last names, e-mail addresses, DOB, and a comment section.
- Maintain a list of friends and e-mail updates to them.

Creating a Friend Strategic Plan might seem like overkill, but we aren't creating the strategic plan to learn how to get friends. We are creating the strategic plan around something we understand so we can relate the strategic-plan elements and internalize the framework. Our goal is to learn how to think strategically; we want to be able to automate the simple strategic plans over time and just focus on our vision. Once we internalize the process of thinking about our goals, strategies, objectives, initiatives, road maps, and projects, we aren't going to have to write them down every time. Your goal is to learn the methodology. Strategically planning the mundane might not seem like fun or terribly interesting, but we need to focus on the process.

The strategic plans you create don't have to be complex; they can be put on the back of a napkin. For large visions, you might want a more complex strategic plan. By the time you are using a more complex strategic plan, you will, or should, have someone maintain it for you.

Alignment

When you are building your strategic plan it is essential to continually test your ideas for alignment with the vision. The time you spend working on initiatives and projects that are not in alignment with your vision takes away from time you could have been working to support your own vision.

You are going to want to develop a habit of continually testing the strategic plan for alignment. During the planning process you might be unsure of the vision or the right strategies you need to realize the vision. When you have completed your strategic plan, go back and review it to make sure there is alignment with your vision. It isn't uncommon for a strategic plan to sway from the initial vision you have defined. This is especially true when you are working on a strategic plan where others are involved. Without the clearly defined vision, even if there is an understanding, there are hidden and not-so-hidden agendas that folks are going to try to work into the strategic plan. Make sure you understand the alignment with the vision; continually testing the alignment with the vision will help you keep the vision in check. It is easy to get off track when you are in the planning process. Stay focused on your vision and the goals you are looking to achieve. Stay on track and achieve the vision you have set before you.

So how do you know if something is in alignment with the vision? A lot of that is subjective; you can look for qualitative signals that tell you that you are no longer on track. If you have a trusted friend or adviser, you could ask him or her to review your plans and ask whether he or she think you are making progress toward the goals you have laid out. You will get a subjective opinion. If the person you ask does not support the vision, then consider the source. But if your friend is someone whom you hold in high regard, then it might make sense to listen to him or her. Or you could take the qualitative approach to seeing if you are in alignment. If your goal is to complete college in four years but you are only taking one credit a semester, then do the math. Your strategic plan is not in alignment with the vision.

For example, let's assume that the vision for the strategic plan is "I have a strong customer base." You define the goals as "Customers repeatedly come back to me," "My customers have a high perceived value," "Customers like the high touch." You come to the defining-of-strategies section. In your strategies, you determine that to get a strong customer base you decide to reduce the interaction with your current customers to focus on getting new ones. The strategy to reduce interaction with your current customers is not in alignment with your goals. If your goal is to have "high touch," then you need to create strategies that support that goal. Or you might need to modify the goals. The takeaway is that when you are building a strategic plan there are interdependencies to each attribute. Ensuring alignment with the strategic plan will give you a better chance to be on your way to achieving your vision.

Ready-to-Use Plans

What would it be like if you could use a strategic plan that was prebuilt for you, and all you had to do was find a strategic plan for a vision that was in sync with your life vision? There are challenges in life that have been solved time and time again—the common challenges have solutions created for them. All you need to do is determine if that strategic plan is in alignment with your vision and implement it. Think about the trade schools, college programs, technical certifications, and most everything you can think of. They have packaged up a strategic plan to help you meet the vision of whatever the program offers. If you want to become a PGA professional, there is a school for that. If you want to be a dentist or nurse, then there is a school for that too. These visions were created by those who found success in their field of expertise. You pay the fee to go to these schools because you like the vision they offer, you find that vision is in alignment with who you are, and as a result you adopt that strategic plan as your own. There is still work you need to do. You will need to make sure the strategic plan is in alignment with your vision; you are going to need to have a "good studies" strategic plan to help you get through the program. Implementing a ready-to-use strategic plan is a time saver and can help you achieve your vision faster than having to discover the strategic plan for yourself.

Building Your Strategic Plan over Time

Building your strategic plan is going to take some time and experience. You are going to take the lessons learned from all your strategies, setting of goals, initiatives, etc., and learn something from the mistakes you made and be able to recreate some of the successes. Building this level of success won't happen overnight. You can get all the guidance you need, but the ultimate decision is up to you. One way to keep the strategic plan fresh is to work through your high-level strategic plans on scratch paper. You can iterate or redo the strategic plan many times before it makes sense to you. Working through the strategic plan with pen and paper can help you think through the decision you need to make. Write down the vision and whos, whats, whens, wheres, and whys. With a validated vision you can move on to the next step.

If working through the examples is something that can help you come up with the right strategy to meet your goals, then why not create multiple outcomes with your strategic plans? A strategic plan is really just a plan; you could have alternate visions that are in alignment with your core values. Considering multiple visions gives you the ability to explore the visions and provides possible outcomes before you make an investment in time or money one way or the other. The more practice you put into creating strategic plans, the better chance you have for starting to think strategically and the better chance that you will have thoroughly thought through your strategic plans and possible outcomes. Thinking through your strategic plan also reinforces the process and encourages muscle memory to kick in and helps you internalize the process. Apply the strategic plan to the simple life visions to prove the strategy or strategic plans and to get yourself into the strategic-thinking mode.

Gaining a Competitive Advantage

By now, it is hoped that you will have come up with some reasons why a strategic plan is relevant for your life and business. The strategic plan has other advantages. The reason we are doing this is that if you are able to think strategically about the challenges and creating strategic solutions, you are going to gain a competitive advantage over those who do not. The competitive advantage is not just about ways to make money but is qualitative as well. Thinking strategically is going to give you a competitive advantage over others. Think about the people in your life whom you most admire or whose accomplishments you are in awe of. Do you think they got to the level they are at by accident or by luck? I would say that they have figured out a system to make them successful.

Vision

THE FUTURE STATE DESCRIBES what you want to accomplish. Your future-state vision can be something that is based on a logical outcome or something that is ideal or the best possible outcome.

To be a strategic thinker, you must think strategically. So how do you become a strategic thinker when you are not given opportunities to do so? Strategic thinkers make big decisions that affect masses of people. You might argue that you have not been given the opportunity but that when you are given the opportunity you will know how to act. That is entirely the wrong attitude; strategic big thinkers do not just wake up one day and make big decisions; they started applying strategic thinking to little decisions long before they made their first big strategic decision.

You are going to only have a few opportunities in life where you really need to think strategically on large decisions. The majority of our time is spent making smaller, less-critical decisions. The choices and the decisions we make all have an impact on our end result or vision. There are lots of opportunities in life to strategically make smaller decisions. If you want to be a strategic thinker, you must start thinking strategically. The best way to do this is apply strategic thinking to your daily life. Pull yourself up from the details of everyday life. Abstract yourself from the details.

You have worked through some very simple examples of how you can start thinking strategically, but how do you start to think about your vision? You might be the person who opens up the menu at a restaurant and spends ten–fifteen minutes poring over the menu. What is the best choice? What do I feel like having for dinner tonight? I am feeling like vegetables—no, I want a meat dish. Perhaps the pasta sounds better. The inability to choose your dinner from the menu shows to some degree that you have a vision for the meal, right? You are worried about having the right meat, the best appetizers, the ambiance, and everything else so that you have a good evening. You are putting lots and lots of thought into the details to meet the vision for the dinner. Everyone can be a visionary, even in just simply picking out a dinner.

Think about sitting down to draw a picture. Take a piece of paper and give it to five adults and ask them to draw a picture. Many times the adults will have an irritated response, such as "I can't draw" or "I am not the artistic type." Are you not the artistic type or is the vision you have of the picture not in alignment with your capabilities? You have a vision for what a picture should look like and are not able to accomplish that vision.

Take the same piece of paper and pencil and hand it to a child and you will get a picture. Why is that? The child has no preconceived notions of what the end result should look like, but the adult does. They know what the vision for a picture should look like and are afraid to try because they have failed so many times before.

Before you can be a visionary, you need to start believing in your ability to see the future. The vision is all about the future state. The vision is where we want to be; it is the end state or ideal place. The vision for the strategic plan is the ideal outcome from the strategic plan. The visions are the grandiose or simple plans and ideas that you have before that reality sets in. Creating a vision requires the optimistic side of you to come out and define the ideal state. The vision statement should be forward looking and based on what you have accomplished from all your hard work. The vision will be unique to your situation.

Allow yourself to reach down deep inside and find that inner child who still can dream big. Does that inner child inside of you think that things are not possible? Can you remember when the inner child did not know that he or she could not accomplish something? That you still exists, and if you want to start thinking strategically, you need to feel the sensation that all those negative thoughts are gone. It is just you; the visions that you have are achievable. You can become the person you want to be.

The only limiting factor is you and the limitations you put on yourself.

You can take the same thinking and apply it to anything you want to try to solve. Once you allow yourself to start dreaming and creating the visions, the process you use to create a small vision is the same one you use to realize big visions. The process you use to create the visions can be applied to business, school, personal life, and pretty much anything you can think of. Everyone's vision might be different, but just think about the possibilities. The vision can be both short term and longer term. The longer-term vision is a composition of what you accomplish in the shorter-term strategic plans.

So what are some of the possible visions? The visions are anything you want them to be.

My visions:
- I advanced in my career.
- I got a pay raise.
- I paid off my car.
- I sold my successful business for a profit.
- I purchase a distressed stock and sold it for a profit.
- I graduated with honors.
- I am a scratch golfer.
- My cholesterol is low for my age.
- I have no credit card debt.

- I have lots of friends.
- My house is paid for.
- I retired early.
- I spend my weekdays with my grandkids.
- I wrote a book.
- I have a job that I love.
- I created a strategic plan for my company.
- I can play the piano.
- I am supersuccessful.
- I make the best cinnamon rolls.

There are so many options for visions of what we want to accomplish that we can become overwhelmed by the possibilities. Part of being a strategic thinker is to know what visions are the best for you to focus on. You need to know which visions are going to get you closer to your life goals. There is only so much time, and depending on where you are in your life your values can affect the vision. The financial options might be the best focus, or you might decide to focus on quality of life. There is going to be a give and take for everything you do. You will need to choose what is important for you. That is something that will not be easy, but the right skills and thinking about your choices will help you make the right decisions.

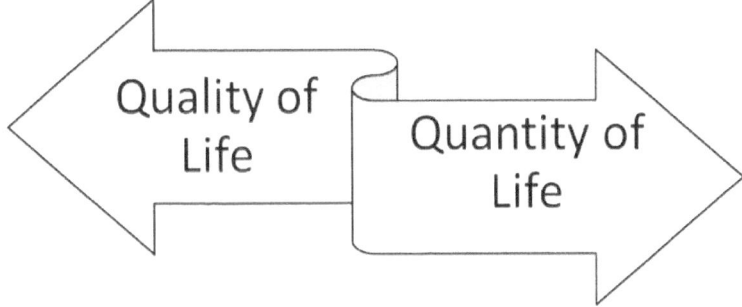

Figure 13 : Quality Versus Quantity

Deciding what your vision is can be challenging. It is especially challenging when you are focused on day-to-day activities. Depending on where you are in life your visions will change. You might be just graduating from college with a ton of school loans and without a strong prospect for a job. The degree you got isn't in vogue and you have recently had to move back into your parents' house. Things are not looking very good, and you are going to have a tough time seeing past the hard time you are experiencing. It is at times like this where you need to turn on the strategic-thinking portion of your brain, forget your current situation, and put down the vision of what you will become.

You might say, "I want to retire at age fifty." Then create the vision: "I retire at age fifty." Your job is to think positively about the situation and not dwell on the dire straits you are currently facing. You may have finished school, be in your mid-forties, and have a spouse, house, children, and a business that is not doing all that you hoped it would. You owe more money on the company than it is worth, times are tough, and you cannot see the light at the end of the tunnel. You must find a way to stay positive and believe in the vision. Your vision is "Run a successful business and sell at a profit." But the business in your vision might not be the one you are currently running.

Who, What, When, Where, Why

Creating your vision is a personal thing. By following the steps below, you should be able to come up with some sample visions. You can accomplish this by answering who, what, when, where, and why, and you can start thinking objectively about your visions. Decide what is important to you to identify a vision that is in alignment with who you are.

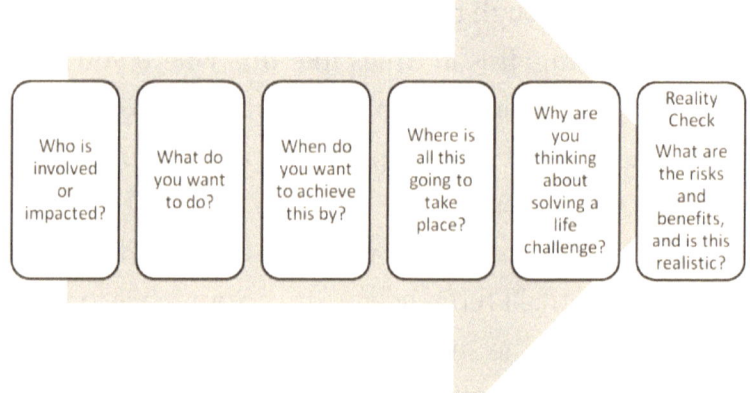

Figure 14 : Asking the Right Questions

Who

Before you embark on a grand vision, you will need to know who will be involved in this vision. If you have a vision that your child will stop taking drugs or you want to keep from getting a divorce, you need to understand those parties involved. If you want to start a successful business, then you might want to consider the partners, if any. Having a vision that is dependent on others adds complexity and will be a more difficult vision to realize than one you have total control over. That is not to say you should not have the vision as your goal, but it is to say that taking on a vision with multiple people involved can be much more challenging.

Having a vision with others involved can increase or decrease your chances for successfully accomplishing the vision. If you have a vision of getting someone to like you and you have done something they would never be able to forgive, then consider the likelihood of realizing the vision. The need for a strategic plan also becomes increasingly important, and you need to find a way to share the vision and define what that strategic plan should look like to help you realize the vision.

What

You are thinking about something, so what is it? What is it that you want to do? You might be trying to solve a big problem or a small problem. This translates to a simple or complex vision. A simple vision could be that you remember the names of people you meet. That is a simple enough vision; this is something that you could create a strategic plan around. Or you might not want to put too much thought into the vision and see something that someone else has done and aspire to accomplish the same goal. Visions like this include going to college or being part of a soccer team. Many people before you have had the vision, and there is a strategic plan you can follow, assuming you have the right grades and can afford the tuition. In the School Strategic Plan there is the vision of "I want to get my degree." That is straightforward enough. Another simpler vision could be "I want to be a good friend" or "I want to transform my business into a market leader."

You could define the "what" as anything you want—to increase sales for the year or be a better father, better mother, or better friend. Whether in business or pleasure, there are things in life we dream about and want to accomplish.

When

When are you planning to achieve this vision? Is it something that you can have completed in a day, a week, a month, or a year? Determine when you want to have this accomplished by; give yourself a date of when you can realize this vision. When you start to define the timeline, you will need to ask yourself some basic questions: *Do*

I have enough time to realize this goal? Is it practical and realistic?

Consider that all things in time are possible, but do you have an unlimited amount of time? You might be forty-five years old and considering a career in the NFL. Well, you might be successful, but when would have been the ideal time to realize this vision? The ideal time would have been thirty years ago, not in your mid-forties. There is only so much time; identifying the "when do I want to realize the vision" can help you determine what a good vision to have is and which is not.

Where

Your odds of accomplishing your vision might increase in some locations versus others. Think about one of the biggest factors in running a successful business—location. Of course there are other factors, but location is an important component. If you can get prime real estate, it is going to cost more, but your chances for getting foot traffic and prospective buyers increases. Location matters in business and also matters in helping you realize your vision.

Think about certain professions that you immediately associate with a certain location. When you think politicians, you think Washington, DC; if you think about models, it's New York or Los Angeles. If you think about technology, Silicon Valley comes to mind. For real estate, you think about the hot spots in the world and the big cities. Realizing your vision might need more than just having the skill and knowledge. You might also need to be in the right place to accomplish your vision. To successfully create your vision, you might need to consider where the highest likelihood of you accomplishing your vision is.

Why

You know what you are planning on doing; now ask yourself why you are thinking about it. Have you been told that you should do it? Is this something you know you have to plan for, such as retirement? Is this something that is going to improve your social life or bring you pleasure? Do you have a talent that needs exploring? If you are seven foot two inches tall and well coordinated, maybe a career in basketball isn't outside of your reach.

In life, you sometimes do things for others or out of habit. Think about all the things you do on a daily basis that are not in your best interest. We are always doing things for others in life, at work, and at home, for parents and friends, to name a few. By asking yourself why you are doing this or why this is important, you can identify what needs to be focused on first. If you can't answer, then why are you doing this—is it worth doing?

Reality Check

Check yourself before you wreck yourself. There are times when your visions might not be realistic and it is time to face the reality of the vision. While we have an amazing ability to accomplish things in life, you need to do a reality check to see if this is something you can accomplish and should do. Is this something that is worth my time and energy to try to pursue? What is the benefit I am going to get out of trying to get to this goal? What is the cost of my investment in terms of time and money? What is the benefit I am going to get out of it?

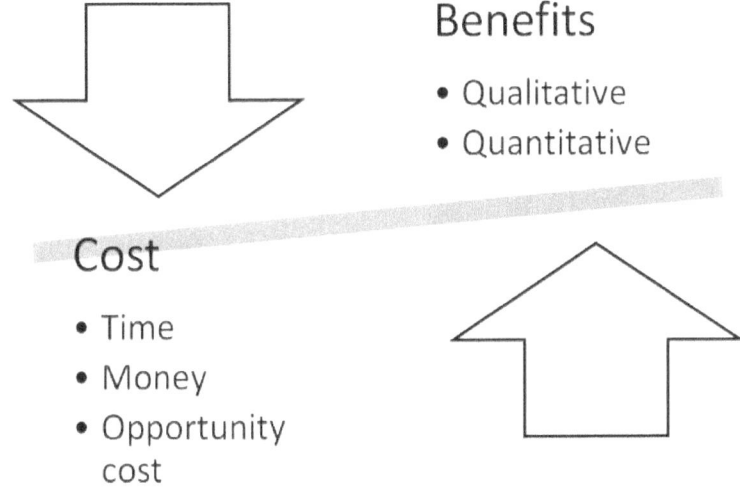

Figure 15: Cost Benefit of Our Decision

Consider the nature of your ambitions and the likelihood that you will accomplish them. In some cases, you need to have intermediate steps to reaching your goal. Consider all the required steps to reaching your goal. If you have a goal of being a surgeon but have not gone to medical school, then consider that the time to realize your goal will increase as well as the number of other strategic plans you will need to create to realize the ultimate vision.

- Who
- What
- When
- Where
- Why
- Reality check

You can use the who, what, when, where, why, and reality check to create the vision for all your strategic plans. This simple process can be used to create all the strategic-plan visions that you have. No matter what vision you create, there is no right or wrong answer. You are unique, and the vision of who you want to be and what you want to accomplish is limited only by your imagination. If you lack the creative ability to come up with a unique vision and you know someone who has achieved the success you want, you can incorporate his vision of how he got to where he is. Copying someone is a sign of flattery. If you are a student looking for a new career or a business who is trying to make a name for herself, there is nothing wrong with interpreting the vision of someone else or another entity and hoping for similar success.

You can think of many examples of when you have copied someone else's vision; for example, in your own family, perhaps you have an uncle or aunt who seemed to have the perfect life, the right number of children, the ideal home, and yearly vacations. Why not emulate his or her success and adopt it for your own? You have heard the phrase "He is following in his father's footsteps." Well, that is a perfect example of following your father's strategic plan. What better way to increase your chances of success in the strategic plan than to interpret the vision and adopt a modified version to suit your needs?

You Are Unique

You have heard that no two people have the same fingerprints. That is pretty amazing; out of the billions of people on the earth there are no two people with the same fingerprints. As with fingerprints, everyone should have a unique vision that is totally his own. And given that your vision is different, how you get there might not be the same either. So while you are creating your ultimate vision or strategic plan, remember that certain paths can have similarities—such as you went to the same school as others or you shared a community or faith with a number of other folks. But your underlying strategic plan might go in directions that others have not nor should they.

Just Create It

A large portion of success is just deciding it is important enough for you to do it. Making the decision to do something can be more difficult than settling down and deciding what you should be working on. You might have gone with someone to a restaurant where she built the place up to be the end all and be all of restaurants, but when she got there she was so struck by the restaurant that she could not decide what to order. You want to be prepared so that when opportunities for you to be successful arise you are prepared to deal with them. Being a strategic thinker can help you make a decision when you are under pressure and need to quickly decide.

To create the vision and strategy of who you want to be, it is important to expand your mind to see what the world has to offer. The best way to do this is to read about other successful people. Think about what you are good at and what gives you that sense of accomplishment. Do some soul searching to see what it is that makes you feel a sense of accomplishment. Do you like to solve problems? Are you an avid reader? Are you mechanically inclined? Have people said you have a great personality? All of these are clues to your future destiny. One thing is for sure: if you do nothing, you will not be able to realize what you dream of. The next step is to define that vision of where you want to be. Are you the next Brad Pitt but are hoping to be recognized while working in the local grocery store in Grand Rapids, Michigan? In all honesty, you might get lucky, but if you don't take action, you will never realize the dreams you have set out for yourself.

You know you are capable of accomplishing great things in this world. You have the skill and ambition; it might just take some planning.

You have heard many times that if you write down your goals you are more likely to achieve them. Before you write down goals to accomplish, you must first ask yourself if the goals you want to accomplish are in alignment with your vision. Accomplishing a goal that is not in alignment is more of a distraction than anything. Your future is not yet defined; you are capable of accomplishing great things.

It is important to visualize who that person is whom you want to become. Start thinking about the future you and where you will be in the next one, five, and ten years. Can you start to visualize what it is that you are going to be? If not, what steps are you going to take to start to define the vision? Are you looking for a career? Perhaps you start reading about all the industries and fields out there. Your vision over time will change, and as your vision changes, you will need to update your strategic plan to meet those goals.

You may have even defined what you want to become. You may have even written down what the future you will look like. With a good idea of what your vision will look like, now is the fun part, determining the goals for getting to that future state. If you decided that in the future self you wanted to be a great cook with two children and you save 10 percent of your money a year with a great job, you should start to break down your vision into the respective categories. If you are going to become that great chef, start to think about how you can realize that vision.

Articulating your vision is one thing, but committing pen to paper and getting that vision written down adds a new dimension. When you commit those ideas to paper, you are saying to yourself, *I can do this*. The act of writing down the vision reinforces it more than saying it. Always try to write down the plan when possible. Building strategic plans is a personal process; it is also an iterative process. The iterative process means that you will work through the process and components in the process multiple times to get to the end result. Ask yourself if what you have learned in the vision section will have any implication on your strategic plan. Do you want to adjust the vision based on what you have learned, or are you still happy with the vision of where you want to be? The vision in some cases is not a realistic vision for you based on physical or mental limitations. You might have had the vision given to you and you wake up one day and realize that you know you really don't want to be this person in the future. *If my outcome is this, then I need to shift the vision.*

Building your strategic plan does not have to be unique to you. There are no rules that say you cannot borrow any ideas or goals from others who are successful. If you find a goal or a strategic plan that appeals to you, just take it as your own. Say your vision is to make a good living; there are a number of strategic plans you could adopt. Consider a trade program or vocational tech program. By completing the trade program and getting a job in the industry, you are realizing the vision associated with the strategic plan. The vision you choose does not have to be one that is unique to you. If you don't have an idea or a strategic plan, borrow one.

Summary

Your vision should be idyllic—the best possible outcome. It should be concise and not have many qualitative or quantitative attributes that describe it. The vision is something you will want to do a reality check on. There are some limitations when it comes time to creating a vision—for example, if our vision includes other people or a physical limitation when it comes to sports. The vision for the strategic plan should give you hope when you think about it. Repeating the vision should give you a feeling that, *Yes I can accomplish this vision.* Examples of nondescript visions include "I am healthy," "I have a successful business," "My family is close," or something like "My yard is well maintained."

Goals

THE VISION IS THE ideal, the utopian high level of what you want to become in your life or business. The utopian vision will most likely be comprised of a series of qualitative goals that define the vision. The goals should be related to your overall vision. Take, for instance, early retirement as the vision. If you said in your vision that you wanted to retire early, the goal would be *how early?* And given that you have retired early, what is the manner in which you want to live? Will you retire at fifty and live in a shelter? Most likely that isn't the case, but if you have a goal of retiring early you should be able to put some sort of qualitative attributes around it.

Your goal(s) for the strategic plan should be the qualitative results based on the vision you defined, meaning they should be in alignment with your vision. Think about the retirement scenario. You might have a goal to retiring at age fifty, but what is the quality of the planned lifestyle? Retirement might be something you have as your vision, but what are some qualitative goals? If your goal is to retire, you might be able to accomplish that today by selling all your assets and moving in with a friend. You eat at a soup kitchen and rely on social services to get by. So if this vision is in alignment, then you are ready to retire today. By defining the goals, you are putting added clarity around your vision. We know at a high level what you want to do or become, but now we know the qualitative attributes of the vision as well.

You can start by considering your vision and writing down the qualitative goals that make it up. Going back to the retirement vision, a goal could be that you are retired but feel financially secure. You might define the goal as having the freedom to go on vacations. You want to live a quality lifestyle and be able to donate to charity. *I want to be able to help my children financially.* Your goal helps define qualitatively what your vision has defined. If you had a vision of having resources during retirement but the strategy was not in alignment with that strategy, you will be disappointed come time for retirement. Your goals should define and support the high-level vision.

The goals you define must be closely in alignment with your vision. As you accomplish your goals, you get closer and closer to realizing your vision. Your goals are not limited to a single attribute but could be multiple attributes in support of the vision. These qualitative attributes can be as few or as many as it takes to realize the vision. The vision is the high-level idyllic and the goals are what we need to accomplish to get there. In this case, the goals are the qualitative attributes with very little detail; you will get more and more specific as you progress through the strategic plan, and you will get more and more tactical. As you can see in the figure below, the goals are qualitative attributes that define the ideal goal of retirement.

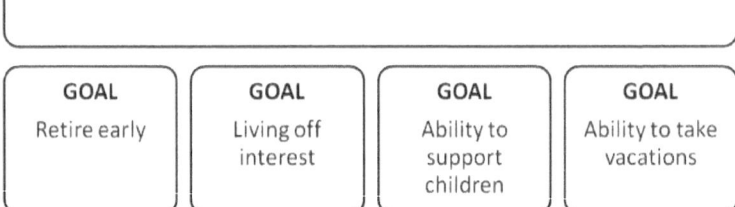

Figure 16: Vision–Goal Relationship

The word *goal* is widely used in everyday terms to mean a number of things. You will hear people say my goal is retirement or my goal is to lose weight. For the purpose of a strategic plan, you will be using goals as the qualitative attributes of a strategic plan. Many times people use *goal* interchangeably with *the vision*, which are two different things. If the goal is idyllic, then it is a vision; if the goal is qualitative, then it is a goal. Be careful when you are using the term *goal*, for the intent of the strategic-plan goal is the qualitative attributes of the vision. The limitation with the goal is that the term *goal* is not multidimensional. We are multidimensional, and the way we think should be congruent with our core being.

Having multiple goals can solve the multidimensional challenges.

Take one of the visions you are thinking about and write it down. Now start to write down all the benefits you can think of, all the benefits that define the vision. If you choose a simple vision such as to have more friends, then think about those friends you have and the friends that you want to have. What are the qualities they have? Are they smart, friendly? Do they do things spontaneously for you? Write down the qualitative attributes of those friends. Are you looking for friends you can just party with, or are you looking for friends that have similar interests? You are the owner of the vision, and you get to take control of the goals and where you want them to go.

If you want to have a group of friends with similar interests, then write down all the interests you can think of. You want friends who are always there for you no matter what. You want friends with whom you feel comfortable sharing your innermost dreams and hopes. Write down the qualities that you are looking to achieve. These are the qualitative goals that if achieved would help you realize your vision.

Say you start thinking about your visions and you decide that one day you want to own your own business. You write down your vision as owning your own business. So is that it? The vision is idyllic. We know very little else about the vision that you are trying to realize. What if you get your wish of owning your own business but since you didn't specify what that business should be like you get a business that has negative cash flow? Now you own your own business, but you have to finance and borrow money from family and friends to keep it running. Is that the kind of vision you intended? If you don't specify the kind of business and describe the qualitative nature of how the vision is to play out, then you might get a business but one that is less than desirable.

By defining goals to support the vision, you can give yourself a clearer picture of what it takes to realize the vision. You want to be able to control as much about the vision as you can. By adding qualitative goals, you will be better able to see the vision that gives you a better chance of accomplishing it. Consider creating qualitative goals for the vision of having a successful business. What would those goals look like—a business in a field that I am passionate about; customers want my goods and services; I operate with high margins; I have the flexibility to shut down and take a week off without loss of income?

You might also want a business that has no overhead so that you can operate from home. Identifying the qualitative nature of the vision and creating goals gives you the information you need to start building a successful strategic plan that is in alignment with the vision.

Evaluate your strategic plan frequently to make sure the goals are in alignment with the vision. After defining the goal attributes of the vision, you should take some time to alter the vision if it is not representative of the goals you have defined, and consequently if you have a goal that is not in alignment with the vision, you should make modification to the vision and goals until they are achievable and in alignment with the vision you have set for yourself. Feel empowered to go back to the vision multiple times to make sure there is an alignment with the goal you have put down. Having alignment of the vision with the goal is imperative to getting one step closer to the vision.

Summary

The goals of the strategic plan is the second layer down from the vision. The goals are the qualitative attributes that define the vision. When you have accomplished all the goals, you have accomplished the vision. Consider the choice of having a vision of weight loss. Goals might include "I feel great," "I get lots of compliments," "People tell me I look good," "My doctor compliments me on my cholesterol." The goals of a strategic plan are 1-n number of goals that should be accomplished to realize the vision.

STRATEGIES

MOST OF YOUR ACTIVITIES so far have been soul searching to get an understanding of what your vision is. You then took the vision to a qualitative level to determine the qualities of the vision that make it unique. The strategies are the courses of action you take to get you one step closer to your goal. Simply put, what do we need to do to accomplish this goal? Strategies are actions implemented to meet our goals. As in everything that you do, you can have a good strategy that gets you close to the goal or a not-so-good strategy that takes you further away from the goal. You need to ask yourself what strategies or activities you can do to get you one step closer to accomplish the goals you defined. There are so many strategies that you can implement that you can sometimes be more effective by consulting someone with domain expertise rather than using trial-and-error strategies. If you are working on a strategic plan that is well defined, such as doing taxes, the better strategy might be to consult a tax adviser rather than trying to do it on your own. Consider looking to others for ideas on which strategies to try. You have been responsible for your own strategies to date, and you may not have gotten you the results you expected. Strategies are, in many cases, the most important aspects of the strategic plan. A successful strategy can propel you fast toward the goals and accomplishing the vision. A poor strategy can push you further and further from the goal(s) you have defined. The strategies you choose are very important to successfully achieve the vision.

In this section, you will want to spend a fair amount of time working through all your options. Consider that there might be more than one way to go about meeting the vision in the strategic plan. If you have a complex strategic plan that is dependent on a strategy, then consider working through smaller strategic plans to get you the practice you need before embarking on a complex, multilayered strategic plan. Keep in mind that many times the secret to a person's success is his ability to effectively execute a strategy that no one has tried before. You need to experiment with strategies in low-risk situations to help you build confidence in your ability to create strategies to meet the goals. You need to think big and reach for strategies that can help you get to the desired end state and realize the vision.

As with the vision and goals, you should feel comfortable proposing multiple strategies to meet the goals. You might find yourself thinking that there is only one way to accomplish the goal you have set out, but if you think about it, there is another way. When you start to think about the other ways to meet the goal, you are strategizing. You are thinking about the different activities you could do to accomplish the same goal. You will need to get past the inclination to think that there is only one way to get from point A to point B when in reality there are multiple ways. There are multiple ways of thinking about solving the problem, and the first one that comes to mind might not always be the best one. Or the first one could be the best strategy and all others might pale in comparison. Choose your strategy well; like the rest of the strategic-plan components it should be flexible enough to be ready for a change.

Consider the vision of you "People think I am smart." You define the goals of "Getting good grades in school," "Doing well on a test makes me feel good." You decide that the strategies to get to this vision are "Cheat on the tests" and "Pay someone to do my homework." In this case there is the moral aspect to test taking. You could realize your vision by using the strategy to "Cheat on the tests." You are the one who has to live with the decisions of the strategies, and while it is true that you could get to the vision of "People think I am are smart," in reality, you are cheating yourself. Accomplishing the goals and vision as defined above, the outcome will only be a façade. Your attempt to leverage the strategic plan you chose will break down because you didn't do the work. You are the one who has to live with your decisions in life.

It is okay to get help with your strategies. It would be fair to say that most strategies are not patented and you can reuse, retool, and repurpose strategies to meet your goals. Perhaps the best way to get help with your strategies is to find a plan whose vision is most similar to the vision you have defined. Find a friend, family member, business partner, or other person who has accomplished a similar goal and ask him or her what he or she did. *I want to know how you did it.* For argument's sake, let's say you have a rich uncle. Everyone knows the uncle is rich, but you don't think to ask how he did it. You have wondered for years and felt that his wisdom was beyond your capabilities and that he would be offended by your request. You cannot be shy about having a vision, goals, and strategies to meet your strategic plan. Just sit down and ask the uncle, "How did you become so successful?" Write down what he did and see if the strategies he used are something you can apply to your vision. People are eager to share their success stories; just ask.

You never know where your best strategy will come from. Just like any type of research, you might get information secondhand or firsthand or you might set up an experiment. Start looking for strategies and they will start coming to you. If you are at a loss as to where to start, a great place is through secondary research online. Do your online homework or go to the library to do secondary research. Pick up a magazine that is pertinent to your vision. If your vision is to be a golfer, then pick up a golf magazine and look at the ads, Google *golf* at your home, or ask a friend with clubs to take you. This all seems like pretty common sense, and it is what the strategic plan does for you. It gives you a framework to be successful with the little successes; you then apply that thinking to bigger and bigger visions.

Let's assume that you are working on a vision to have a career or to get people to like you; consider an Internet search. Take the recommendations and break them down into the various components. As you read the articles, think about the recommendations. Are they qualitative or quantitative? Are there timelines or recommendations on how to achieve the vision in the article? What is the author telling you? Does he or she describe the goal, the initiative? Are there objectives or a predefined strategic plan that you could incorporate into your own strategic plan? As you go through your life you will want to start classifying all the information you are getting from people. When you do this, you will start to see how people are thinking. By absorbing and classifying the information you are getting, you should be able to identify a strategic thinker from a goal-oriented thinker and from a tactical one. It is simple to subscribe to blogs, trade magazines, and other periodicals that relate to the vision. Read the material and filter the material; ask others if they have tried the strategy and if it worked for them. There might be a great-sounding strategy out there that looks wonderful on paper but in practice does not work. Have an open mind when getting your information. A strategy that worked for someone else might not work for you. It is also possible that a strategy you tried that did not work at first will work with a couple of changes. This is where the experience you gain from thinking strategically is going to help you over time.

Always get advice from a professional. Getting professional help from a consultant could be just the tactic to help give you the advice to get you on your way. Think about what consultants do—they have specific knowledge in a specific area. They are the subject-matter experts in their area and have been successful at figuring out the strategic plan for their area of expertise. Take their recommendations as input, just like secondary research, and break the information into the categories of vision, goals, strategies, objectives, initiatives, road maps, and projects. The information they give can also give you a perspective on how they think. Are they thinking strategically or do they have the answer before you finish describing the challenge?

Consider the Retirement Strategic Plan. Think about the strategies you could use to meet the goals of retiring early, living off interest, supporting children, and taking three vacations a year. To meet those goals, you might say that your strategy is to purchase lottery tickets. Purchasing lottery tickets is a perfectly viable strategy, but what is the likelihood of you meeting the goal? You could research lottery sales and determine for yourself if purchasing lottery tickets is a good way to plan for retirement. Do your homework on the strategies to see if they are viable. Here are two case studies of mega lottery winners.

Strategy: Win the lottery

- A sixteen-year-old won 1.91 million euros. That is enough money to support your retirement goals. The challenge here was that she didn't save the money. She spent it on vacations, homes, shopping, and multiple breast implants. After losing all that money, she attempted suicide twice.
- **Outcome**: At age twenty-two, she is working as a maid to support her family.
- Another winner won eighteen million dollars in a Missouri lottery in 1993. She started contributing the money to politics, education, and the community.
- **Outcome**: She ended up with nothing.

The list of people who have won the lottery and are not retired is staggering. Your strategy of winning the lottery might give you a quick glimpse into the strategy of just winning the lottery. For starters, it is next to impossible to do, and second, even if you win the lottery, you do not have a very good chance of keeping the money you won.

And this applies not just to lottery winnings but to every large payment you get. Consider talking to a financial adviser; ask for his strategy on building enough wealth to meet your goals. You can learn a lot from people who have been in your shoes before. Ask if they had the chance to redo their decision what they would do.

Strategy: Save enough money to retire early

I am going to save 10 percent of my money and all my bonuses in a separate account. This strategy might seem like a fairly good approach to meeting your retirement. You are doing exactly what your grandparents suggested—saving your money for a rainy day. The challenge is that putting your money in a typical savings account might get you to your goal of retiring, but without adequate leverage you might not ever be able to meet the goals you specified.

Check back to make sure the strategy you go with is in alignment with the vision and will support the goals. In the retirement example, there is a strategy, but without the goals defined we do not know if it is in alignment with the vision. The ultimate strategies that you decide to go with might change as you progress through the strategic plan. Strategies do not always work. Keep in mind that the strategic plan is iterative, and we need to constantly go back to it to determine if it is in alignment and if we are meeting our goals. You are still going to be at a fairly high level at this point.

Assume you have a vision and goals defined. The vision is retirement, and the goals are to retire early, live off interest, support your children, and take vacations. With a defined vision and goals, you can put together your strategy to meet that vision.

In the figure below, you will see that you have some strategies to meet the vision of early retirement. Notice how the strategies are pretty high level. We do not put too many restraints on setting the expectations on the strategy. This is for a reason; you do not want to set the expectations too low or too high. Your strategies should be in alignment with the vision, support the goals, and be abstract enough that you can further define them later on in the process.

Strategies: to Meet the Goals

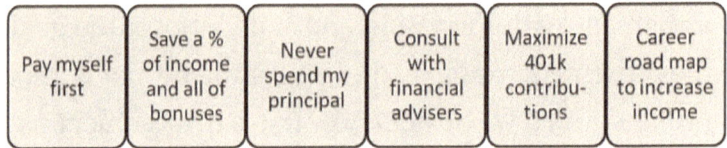

Figure 17: Retirement Strategy

You might have other strategies as well that you could market, such as to buy options or invest in foreign exchanges and get a Forex account. As you can see, there are many strategies you can employ to meet the goals you have set for yourself. Who is to say that one will work or not? At this point, keep the creative juices flowing; the only commitments you are making are the ones on paper. You can strategize all day long and there is no effort needed to put those strategies into motion. Creating the strategies to meet your goal can be fun; it is the "What if" game. What if I did *blank,* such as what if I gambled all my money on red at the table in Vegas?

Evaluate your strategies as you build your strategic plan and evaluate the strategies to meet your vision. Your strategies are going to give you more insight into the reality of you realizing the vision. Check to make sure your strategies are in alignment with the overall vision. You can also do a reality check to see if the strategies are something you can accomplish. The ideal strategy to get you to your vision and goal might be too overwhelming or cause hardship. This is your strategic plan, your vision; you have the power to change.

Summary

When we were little, we were always looking for strategies and ways to do things. Recall asking your mother and father for ways to tie your shoes or for help on a homework assignment. As we get older, we become more likely to make our own decisions and less reliant on others. When you are looking at strategies to meet your goals in life, would it not be in your best interest to have as many as possible to choose from? The amount of information in the world is tremendous. Part of becoming a strategic thinker is to be able to filter the strategies that come to you. Learn to ask questions about the strategies. They are not always right for the vision you have. A perfectly good strategy that is not in alignment with your vision could hurt your chances of attaining your vision.

Building strategies isn't an exercise you need to do in a vacuum. How would you know all the possible strategies without doing some level of research? You might determine the strategies by hiring a consultant or by talking to family and friends or by trial and error. The truth of the matter is that when you pick the right strategy you can meet your goal potentially sooner; choose the wrong strategy and you will lose time that could put you far enough behind that you will never meet your goals.

OBJECTIVES

UP UNTIL THIS POINT in the strategic plan, you have been defining the high-level vision, goals, and strategies. You have been creating statements at a high level that are fairly abstract. Now is the time to kick your tactical brain into overdrive. Now the objectives are more concrete—they are measurable results that describe the strategy milestones you defined. Unlike the qualitative nature of the strategies, the objectives are quantitative. This is the place in the strategic plan where you start to quantify your strategies.

Objectives: to Meet Strategy Milestones

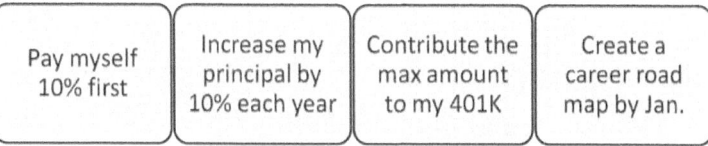

Figure 18: Retirement Strategy

- What are the objectives you must meet to start realizing the vision?
- How are you going to meet the strategies, goals, and ultimate vision you have set for yourself?

Objectives should be specific and measurable. These objectives should include a date, a time, and a place when you will accomplish them. Using the example of retirement, you know you will need to put a dollar figure on how much you should have saved and by when. If you are forty years old and have a vision of retiring at age fifty, you will need to set objectives to get there. Using online calculators and talking to financial advisers or friends, start to work through the scenarios. If I plan on retiring in ten years, I first need to know how much money I will need to meet my goal. So assume you need one million dollars to retire. Now you have a measurable objective that you are trying to reach. You can take those objectives and revisit the strategy and ask yourself which strategy is going to get me one million in ten years. You can check the alignment with the objectives and your strategies.

A way to do this would be to take your strategic plan and go to a financial adviser and sit down for a discussion. This is one of the strategies discussed above. During the discussion, the adviser asks you your income, how much you have saved so far, and a number of other questions. He asks if your house is paid for and what stocks and bonds you have in your name. He will run off and create a scenario for you. He might create multiple scenarios to give you a best case, worst case, and most likely. He might come back and say that based on your retirement needs you need to have fifty thousand dollars a year in passive income. He might say that you won't want to be too risky so assume you are getting about 5 percent return on investment. This means that in ten years' time you will need to have one million dollars in savings.

He looks at you and sees that you have a life insurance policy and fifty thousand dollars in savings. He pulls out his financial calculator and starts figuring. The market has been pretty good, so we will assume a 15 percent return on investment over the next ten years. He types in your current savings of fifty thousand, the one-million-dollar future value, and between a 10 percent and a 15 percent return on investment. He comes back to you saying, "Congratulations. If you could just put away about fifty to sixty-five thousand dollars per year, in ten years you will have a million dollars that you can start drawing on. You will need to save 500 to 650 thousand dollars over the next ten years." Your heart rate quickens and you feel suddenly let down. How are you going to come up with that kind of money? He pulls out the calculators and says, "If you put away between fifteen and twenty-one thousand dollars per year you might be able to retire, but you won't be able to live the lifestyle you had in your strategic plan." Perhaps that is something you can do and is one possible alternative. Or you may want to stick to your guns and keep the objective previously discussed with the adviser. You might even go get a second opinion. There might be other strategies you can do that this adviser isn't thinking about.

The point of this exercise is to identify the objectives that you must achieve to reach your goal. To get to the goal of retirement, we have a quantitative number we now can put into our strategic plan—fifty to sixty thousand dollars per year in savings. We also can figure out how much we should have in two years, three years, five years, etc. You have measurable objectives that you can use throughout the course of the strategic plan to see if you are on track.

You now have some choices with your strategic plan. You can do a couple of things. The first is to change the goal. You ask the adviser what it would take to retire in twenty years and have the one million dollars in the bank. Or you can stick to the goal to finish the Retirement Strategic Plan and create another vision and strategic plan to support your goal of saving fifty to sixty thousand dollars per year. Be prepared for the good and bad news; things won't always work out the way you had planned. The bad news will come with the good. When you get good or bad news, be patient and ask the right questions. Becoming a successful strategic thinker takes experience in solving strategic problems. To solve the problems and think through the right choices, you have to keep a level head, be patient, and keep calm, knowing that it will work out for the best.

You can practice your way into being able to solve the challenges presented in your strategic plan and learn how to solve the smaller problems in a strategic manner. If you start applying your strategic vision to even the smallest of challenges, you will program your brain to solve in a strategic way. You have a lot of tools at your disposal to find a way to solve these challenges.

- You can ask family and friends for suggestions.
- You can seek out someone who has been successful in achieving your vision or goal.
- You can talk to a professional.
- You can search on the Internet.
- You can get magazines or blogs related to your vision.

You do not have to solve the problem all by yourself. Lean on the lessons learned from others and on your own gut feeling. You do have to put in the time to frame the challenge or vision you are looking at realizing. To be able to solve a problem, you must first identify what the problem is. Now is the time to put in writing the milestones you need to meet your goals.

As you start to put the objectives/milestones in place, you should say, *Do these objectives make sense? Do my strategies support the milestones and objectives?* You might also have strategies that take a huge time commitment.

Or the strategy might not be an option for you. Did you say that you want to retire early but also want to be able to take vacations whenever you choose? These goals you have defined all have implications. When building your strategic plan it is imperative that you go back and level set your expectations. What are realistic goals, strategies, and objectives versus those that are pie in the sky?

Summary

Your objectives should be quantitative and measurable. This means that you should have an easy time going back and determining if you met the objectives or not. With a qualitative goal you may or may not know to what degree you achieved the goal. With an objective, you should be fairly certain. You should create an objective where you can go back and measure the delta between where you were in the current state and in the new future state with little to no ambiguity.

Setting and creating the objectives is entirely within your control. This is your vision. You set the bar as high as you want or set the bar low. The objectives are yours to set as you please. The one caveat to setting the objectives is that if you set them too high and do not meet them, you will be disappointed, and consequently if you set them too low and achieve them there is really no challenge in that. So think carefully about your objectives, about what is realistic for you. Setting the objectives can impact your vision. Be prepared to defend your vision. If the vision is so important to you, then the objectives can be reached; you are just going to need to be creative in defining them.

INITIATIVES

THE INITIATIVES ARE THE broad actions that are going to help you accomplish your strategy objectives. The activities might work once or work indefinitely until you meet your desired vision. An initiative that is in support of the "save a percentage of your income" strategy could be to take a percentage of your paycheck and put it into a saving account. This action of putting some of your earnings into a savings account supports the strategy of "save a percentage of your income." These are broad actions that will get you a little closer to the objectives that you defined.

Initiatives: Activities to Accomplish Strategies

Strategy: Save a portion of my income
- Initiative 1:   Use coupons and pocket the money saved
- Initiative 2:   Create separate checking account

Figure 19: Initiatives Example

Using retirement as the example, assume a vision of retirement, a goal of early retirement, a strategy to save money, and an objective of retiring in ten years. You could create an initiative to start clipping coupons. If you were able to save 20 percent on your grocery bill, you could take that 20 percent and put it into a savings account that would support the strategy to meet the objectives that support the goal to realize the vision. You could set up other initiatives that support the strategy to save money, such as reducing your eating-out expenses. For example, you could only take the kids to dinner when they have "children can eat free" specials and put the difference in your savings account. You could start using coupons. These initiatives that you are starting are the broad actions that you can do to support your objectives defined by the strategy.

Thinking more about the retirement vision and your goals of retiring early, you could start an initiative to learn more about investing. This could be accomplished by joining an investment club or by reading the money section of your favorite paper. Joining an investment club to get a better understanding about investments would support the objective you defined earlier. There are trade magazines and journals you can subscribe to, or perhaps you could get alerts and advice from online groups or, more importantly, seek out those who have retired successfully and ask them what they did. While you are thinking about meeting the objectives defined by the strategies, there are endless actions you can take to get you further toward your goal.

During the strategic-planning process, you might come up with a number of initiatives and you aren't sure whether they are going to impact the objective. It is okay to have more initiatives than you need. You can always eliminate initiatives later on in the process. It is better to have more initiatives so you can weigh the costs and benefits than fewer. The strategic-planning process is a way for you to develop a plan. As you develop the plan, the initiatives you thought possible could be too difficult or might not support the overall vision you have set for yourself.

Strategic planning is an iterative process, and you will need to continually revisit your plan and check on its progress. You might be a couple months into an initiative and a life event happens, or you might find out that the initiative is taking too much time and will not have the same effect you'd hoped for. You are in control and can correct the course; this is your strategic plan, and you can determine what is important to work on and what is not. You might even decide that defining a vision is not for you and that it takes too much work. Then you are empowered to switch that vision.

Summary

Initiatives are a series of actions to meet objectives to support the strategy objectives. This means that you still do not want to be too specific in the details of how you are going to accomplish every little objective. The strategic plan sets the direction; the strategic plan provides guidance. The implementation of the strategic plan might have subtle differences. Initiatives could also be a program that you choose to implement to meet the strategy objectives.

- What initiatives do you need for your vision?

Road Maps

Road Maps: Time-Sequenced Activities

> Road maps: Save a portion of my income
> - Road map 1: Enroll in a financial management program
> - Road map 2: Work with financial adviser on retirement plan
> - Road map 3: Fifteen-year mortgage

Figure 20: Road Map Example

ROAD MAPS ARE INITIATIVES with a time-sequenced component to them. An initiative can be executed in any order, but a strategic plan has a beginning, middle, and an end, or something similar to that. A road map has a logical order—you must do A first, B second, and C third. You can have initiatives that are outside of a strategic plan and ones that are time-sequenced within a strategic plan.

You could take a strategic plan, declare it a road map, and link it to another strategic plan. The strategic plan you are working on now is a piece to a large puzzle. It all depends on how complex the problem is that you are trying to solve and whether you need to take a multidimensional approach to solving it. Some examples of ready-to-use road maps that are based on proven strategic plans are

- getting a college degree;
- writing a book; and
- paying off your house.

If you have a home, you most likely have time-sequenced initiatives (a road map) that you are using to pay off the house. You wanted to purchase a house but did not have the cash to purchase the home, so the strategy you used was a mortgage. When you get a mortgage, the broker asks you what term you want. Do you want a ten-, fifteen-, or thirty-year note? The mortgage you choose has an implication on your vision, whether you know it or not. If you maxed yourself out on the mortgage payment and barely qualified for a thirty-year mortgage, you inadvertently pushed out the reality of owning your home in ten years. The choices we make every day have an impact on our road maps. Let's say you defined the goal to pay off the mortgage in fifteen to thirty years. To accomplish the vision you have an objective of paying one payment per month along with a time-sequenced initiative called a payment that you make to the mortgage company. You might not have qualified for 100 percent financing, so you used a strategy of putting 20 percent down on the home. Road maps are used every day in everything we do.

Road maps, for that matter, could also have a vision, goals, strategies, initiatives, other road maps, and projects. That is the great thing about the strategic-planning process: you can tie everything together into a logical unit or separate them into discrete units. For the purpose of learning the process, it will be easier to keep them simple, for now. But for more complex strategic plans, such as a Life Strategic Plan, you can incorporate other road maps. Or the road maps can be time-sequenced initiatives in place. When you go to high school that is a time-sequenced initiative—you are going to go to school for approximately four years. Think of the trade schools or certifications classes you could take. These are all time-sequenced initiatives that have their own life cycle or mini-strategic plans to help meet the broad-stroke initiatives.

Summary

Road maps are used all throughout our lives; they are visible in every aspect of your life. You are driven by them and just don't realize it. By being able to identify the initiatives we have in place, you can start to control your destiny. What are the road maps in your life today? Which of those road maps are in alignment with the vision of who you want to be? By actively looking at the things you do in life, you can guide your own destiny.

Projects

Projects: Organization and Execution of Initiatives

> Projects: Accomplish my Initiatives and Roadmaps
> - Project 1: Update mortgage payment plan, and start making payments
> - Project 2: Setup meeting with Financial Advisers

Figure 21: Creating Your Projects

THE PROJECTS ARE WHAT you need to do to realize the vision; they are the implementation plan, so to speak. The projects are what you will be using to organize all your initiatives into something meaningful so that you can start to realize the vision. Once you define and implement the strategic plan, it becomes an entity all to itself. The initiatives, on the other hand, are not time sequenced, so we need a way to organize them. We do so by organizing them into projects. The collective unit (project) is created to attain one of our objectives or milestones. For the simple strategic plan, you might not even need to create a project—you just implement the initiative. Say you have a vision of paying off your house. You defined an initiative of paying more on the house. You got a lump sum of money from work for a job well done. The project is simple—take the money from your checking account and pay down the principal; that's it—you are done.

Or say your vision was to have your house paid off in fifteen versus thirty years. You determined that the strategy of putting extra money toward your house would help you meet that goal. Through the strategy section, you spoke to a mortgage broker who said that paying down the principal every month would you help you meet the goal. You had a mortgage of one hundred thousand dollars, with a payment of $534 a month. The broker said that if you paid $787 a month you would be able to pay off the home in fifteen years. You had the money available, so your projects are to update the Mortgage Payment Strategic Plan to add an extra $253 extra per month to the mortgage.

By defining a vision, goals, strategies, objectives, initiatives, road maps, and projects to realize the vision of living in a house that is paid for, all you need to do now is implement that project. If you stick by the project, you will live in a house that is paid off in fifteen years rather than thirty. With solid projects in place that are in alignment with the vision, you have a much better chance of accomplishing the goals that are going to get you close to your vision. With your project in place, you now have a systematic way to go about realizing your goal of owning your home in fifteen years. You can forget about thinking about paying off your home or wishing your home was paid off.

The projects you define are the activities that organize the initiatives that will ultimately meet the objectives you have defined. At the project level, this is the most tactical you are going to get. These activities, once met, will take you to the vision or closer to the vision. If your objective was to pay off your house in ten years and you owe one hundred thousand dollars with a 6 percent loan, what payment would you need to make to pay that house off in ten years? You might also want to define the amount of money you should be putting away each month.

Summary

The projects are the last piece to your strategic plan; they are the glue, the activities that you will use to stitch the strategic plan together to be able to implement it. Your project or projects take the initiatives and bundle them up into logical units to be able to accomplish the objectives and, in turn, the strategy milestones.

BUILDING YOUR STRATEGIC PLAN

BUILDING YOUR STRATEGIC PLAN is going to take a mastery of the strategic-plan principles. For starters, you are going to need to understand each of the seven areas of a strategic plan. You need to understand vision, goals, strategies, objectives, initiatives, road maps, and projects. You should understand what each of the seven areas is, understand what each one's definition is, and be able to cite examples. You might even start by just identifying and mapping what you do in your life in terms of the strategic plans. Ask yourself, *What is my vision? What are the goals I have? Do I have strategies in place? What are my objectives? Am I following a strategic plan today?*

Having a strategic plan already built for you would be ideal. If the strategic plan was already built, it would be simple. All you'd need to do is execute the projects and implement the strategic plans that support the initiatives that meet the objectives based on the strategies that will give qualitative results toward the goal that accomplishes the vision. When you are able to implement the project successfully, then you are realizing the vision. You can successfully implement many of the strategic plans in your life. The challenge comes when you are trying to accomplish a life goal. There are emotions involved in the strategic plan. If you aren't getting the support you think you need, your vision might be very difficult to achieve. Then add to this the fact that, like people, no two life strategic plans are the same.

You also might find that people don't like to follow in the footsteps of others anyway. Consider the feeling of being compared to a brother or sister in class. The teacher would say, "You are following in your brother's footsteps." For some it is okay; for others the thought of being just like a brother or sister is like nails on the chalkboard. "I am nothing like them," you mutter under your breath. Those being copied have a similar reaction—quit copying me! You will get in trouble for copying in school, so why would you want to copy the strategic plans of others? Ask yourself, *Is my pride more important than my happiness or being successful?* Sometimes it is okay to follow in someone's footsteps. That means you will have an easier time realizing the vision; that person has done the hard work for you.

Every day you need to make strategic decisions that are going to impact your life. For this simple fact, it is important that you internalize the process of creating the strategic plan. You must start thinking in the ways of the strategic plan. It may sounds daunting, but with a little practice it becomes like muscle memory, or strategic-plan memory. You will start thinking strategically about your life and the things you need to accomplish in life. And, over time, you will find the success you have wanted and yearned for.

Building the strategic plan begins by understanding what each of the areas in the plan are. Understand the definitions; be able to discern your goals versus initiatives. If you say, "I want to lose five pounds," is this a vision or perhaps a goal? Or is this an objective because it is quantitative? The statement is specific, so you would not want to use this as a vision. Let's compare the statement "Lose five pounds" to the goal. In reviewing the definition of goals, we see that they are qualitative results. So the statement does not fit into the goal. When you lose five pounds it is a result, so the loss of five pounds would be considered an objective. If you have more to lose, you could lose five pounds in four months and ten pounds in eight months.

It might seem that we are splitting hairs by being too cautious with the choice of words. Deleting from the statement "Lose five pounds of weight" could change the statement from "Lose five pounds of weight" to "Lose weight." By simply omitting the five pounds we could now easily move the phrase to the vision or perhaps a goal to support the vision. It is important that you choose your words carefully. It might not seem like a big deal, but you want to start thinking strategically. The strategic thinkers are the ones who run the world's business and are the most successful. Getting in the practice of choosing your words carefully will help you differentiate between the various levels, so when you hear an idea you can filter it. Filtering it will give you the ability to identify other strategic thinkers.

With a solid understanding of what each of the areas means, you can now start to practice creating strategic plans. Start with something small; this is going to save you grief and build your confidence by successfully getting a small strategic plan done. The bigger ones will come in time, or if you can master the thought process, you won't even need to write down a word; the strategic-planning process will be part of your daily routine.

Another way to do this is to jot down your ideas throughout the day or week. At the end of the period of time you choose, say a day, classify the thoughts into categories. You might have said, "I wish I had a million dollars." Ask yourself where that statement would fit. Or you might have said, "I wish I had a new car." Write down the statement and then build the rest of the strategic plan based on that statement. If you said you wished you had a million dollars, then decide what it is for. Getting a million dollars is an "objective" because it is descriptive, but what is that million dollars for? What vision is the million dollars going to help you achieve? Do you owe the IRS a million dollars? Is a million dollars the money you need to retire? What do you plan on doing with a million dollars? By writing down the objective, you can build the strategic plan.

Objective:	A million dollars
Vision:	IRS is paid off
Goal:	Pay bill to IRS
Strategy:	Wish
Objectives:	One million dollars
Initiatives:	Wish upon a star; make a wish in a wishing well
Road maps:	n/a
Projects:	Plan a trip to find wishing wells and make wishes

As you can see by creating the strategic plan, "I wish I had a million dollars" isn't much of a strategic plan. It isn't getting you close to thinking strategically. Those thoughts like "I wish" and "I hope" aren't going to help you meet your goals. They might make you feel better, but if all your thoughts are that way you can see by the strategic plan that you are not thinking strategically.

As you talk with people at work or with your family, start to jot down their statements. How are they thinking? Ask them, "What would you like to be in five years?" or "What are your plans?" List their statements. Put the statements down on paper and put them into the appropriate category on the strategic plan. Are they thinking strategically? Perhaps you overheard someone in your family saying, "Joe got a new iPod. His parents are rich. I wish I had rich parents."

Take those statements from the family member and start to reverse-engineer a strategic plan.

Vision:	Born to rich parents
Goal:	Get what you want
Strategy:	Get reborn
Objectives:	Get an iPod
Initiatives:	"Use your imagination"
Road maps:	n/a
Projects:	n/a

As you can see, these statements are not strategic. You are better off not wasting your time listening to people who wish or hope for things; they are not thinking strategically. And if all their words are of that nature, then you are not dealing with a strategic thinker. They are not thinking logically or rationally. Most likely the statement was made out of desperation for something they will never be able to achieve. Keep an ear open for this type of speech; you will find it every day in the workplace and in school interactions. That type of speak might make you feel good, but it won't help you get to your objectives.

As another way to find like-minded people who believe in the strategic-planning process, have a strategic-plan study club where you can share ideas and strategic plans about how to meet your goals. It might sound sophomoric to do, but why not? We go to an accountant for help with taxes and a doctor when we are sick. Why not go to your group for help in thinking strategically? If you are able to identify those with similar interests, your chance of becoming good at building strategic plans improves. Plus, do you really want to build strategic plans all alone in your home? You will get so much more satisfaction when you have someone who understands and shares your vision. You are working together to understand and validate each other's strategic plans. How good would you feel when you are able to say to your buddy that you met your goals? You call them up and say, "Hey, I finished the book I was working on. Remember when I created that vision?" Or call up your children and say, "Dad quit his job today." After the gasping and questions about how you are going to live, you calmly say that the plan worked—I was able to retire early we are going to be just fine.

The strategic plan does take one investment that is more precious than any. That investment is your time. The more time you spend on the strategic plan, the better your chance for mastering the material and becoming a strategic thinker. This means that you will want to set aside time to work on the strategic plan and skills. One of the ways you can start is to set aside a Saturday afternoon to work through the strategic plan. If you are learning the skills, you can practice creating daily strategic plans from your thoughts or the ideas others have discussed with you throughout that day. If you are starting a bigger initiative, then perhaps you want to have a more formalized meeting with all those stakeholders involved in the vision.

If your vision was to have a happy family life, then to have a successful strategic plan you will need to get your family's buy-in. Invite them to a library or coffee shop for a couple of hours to talk about the vision, goals, and strategies you could undertake to make life more enjoyable.

Living the Strategic Plan

Want-to Gene

TO BE A STRATEGIC thinker and be someone who can accomplish your goals isn't as simple as creating a strategic plan and you are there. The strategic plan is going to take a time investment. You will need to modify your daily activities. Foremost in successfully adopting and building strategic plans is that you have the want-to gene. The want-to gene was not handed down to everyone, but if you have it, you will know. There is always a persistent voice inside your head telling you what to do. Those starting to think strategically might encourage those with the want-to gene to be careful.

Secondary to the want-to gene is that you have to have some organizational skills. They don't have to be much, but set aside the time to think about your strategic plans. Set aside time when you can think about where you are today and where you want to be. You will need to be organized enough to take the time to think about the strategic-plan creation and maintenance. Depending on the complexity of the strategic plan, you might spend five minutes a day. Make the time the same every day. You might do it before work or after breakfast; if you are a late-night person, then do it right before bed.

To accomplish the goals defined in the strategic plan, it takes time to do the projects and time to get your initiatives done. For this, you must be able to prioritize your time so that you can spend time on the initiatives that are going to get you to your goals. With discipline, you can think more strategically and you can accomplish your goals and dreams, but it will take discipline to revisit your strategic plan(s) and update when necessary.

Think about the steps we took to create the strategic plan to pay off the house in fifteen years. It might seem like a long way to go to get a paid-off home, but you will now start to think strategically when it comes to purchasing a home in the future. Also, when you come across other capital investments where you require a payment option you might think back to the House Strategic Plan and apply the findings to what you did to pay off the home early. If you can pay off your home, why not your car, your credit cards, or whatever other debt you have? When it comes time to think about money and the time value of money, you have a better understanding from a strategic perspective of how it works.

Take the retirement example we wrote about in a prior section. Understanding the time value of money and the strategic plan, we know that when we apply more funds to the objective we are able to realize the goal faster. We also identified how we can make changes in our lives to be able to afford the initiative we are going after.

After you have finished defining the strategic plan, the next step is to find a way to realize the strategic plan. The beauty of thinking strategically about your vision is that you can determine how to manage the projects and initiatives you have defined. Incorporate them into your daily planner or electronic calendar, commit it to memory, or put it on sticky notes in the bathroom.

Revisiting Your Strategic Plan

You can define the greatest vision and have super strategies to get to realize the vision. But if you do not have an organized way to go about finishing the projects that will accomplish the objectives defined, then it is a moot point to create a vision. How you manage and automate your strategic plans is up to you. If you have a business with a number of employees, you can delegate to the employees to complete the projects. You might look for volunteers to help realize the vision.

Maintenance

Building your strategic plan is going to be an iterative process. You can define your vision, goals, strategies, objectives, initiatives, road maps, and projects, but life can, and does, happen. It is important to come back to your vision and strategic plan regularly to see how you are doing. Are you meeting the goals you have defined?

Did you
- get a new job;
- lose your job;
- have a baby; or
- get married?

All these life-changing events can have an impact on your strategic plan. Life lessons must be applied to your strategic plan. As you progress through the strategic plans of your life, be aware of what is working for you and what is not working. You must be able to identify and modify the plan based on your experiences. You might have the seemingly perfect strategic plan and feel that there is nothing that will make you change your dream. You might come across a different strategic plan that is just as powerful, if not more powerful, than the one you envisioned. You might have a feeling that you are destined for greatness but are not sure what that greatness would look like. Or perhaps the vision of greatness you had is not in alignment with where you should go. Identify what is working and what is not and be ready to shift your strategic plan.

Discipline

Creating the strategic plan is only the first step; it is important to have the discipline to stick with your strategic plan. There are temptations all around you that will try to make you veer off course. With a clear strategic plan you will be more likely to meet your objectives, but you may need to have course corrections from time to time. Realize that your strategic plans take determination and an internal strength to stay the course. Set up the time you are going to work on the strategic plan in advance. The time could be only five minutes where you think about the strategic plans and where you want to go next.

The more success you enjoy, the more you will find that it is important to have systems in place to support the strategic initiatives and vision that you have created. Keep yourself focused on the strategic initiatives; you want to drive the vision, strategy, and objectives. You alone are the one who is going to be the controller of your destiny. Keep thinking strategically. It might become fun to start to implement all these projects you create, but it is better to share the responsibilities. Enjoy the success and focus on what is important and not the tactical day to day, unless of course you have reached enough success. Then only focus on the tactical. It is, after all, your strategic plan; you have the ability to focus on what you want.

Writing a strategic plan does not guarantee success. Your goal with writing strategic plans is to help you start to think strategically about accomplishing your goals and visions. The more strategic plans you write, the more strategic in nature your thinking will become. Your first strategic plan might lead to wild success, or perhaps you will create a strategic plan and get no financial gain out of it. That does not mean that the strategic plan was not successful. You will be driven to even greater successes, and next time you try you will know what to do differently. You will have learned a lot from the experience, and the little feeling of success you got by accomplishing your little goals will push you to accomplish larger and more complex goals. And at some point you will be the strategic thinker, the one who calls the shots and drives the vision of where things should be.

Ex-Post-Facto Strategic Plan

Who says your strategic plans have to be based on future events? One of the ways you can learn more about how you think is to look back on a successful event or accomplishment and build a strategic plan. Your accomplishment might have been short-lived or fleeting, but you still accomplished something that made you feel good about yourself. Looking back on the accomplishments of the past and documenting what you did, write down the vision you accomplished that will give you insight into the strategic-planning process. It will also familiarize you with the strategic-planning process. Think about your accomplishments. Did you graduate from high school when you didn't think you could? Were you able to keep the weight off before but not now? Did you have tremendous success on a team? You can learn about the future by reflecting on the past.

Managing Your Success

You have spent the whole book thinking about how to think strategically. Thinking strategically can put you in a position to execute the activities that will get you to your vision, but thinking strategically alone will not get you to the end state or vision. The more success you have, the more there will be to manage. As your success grows, you will need people to support you in the effort.

It is important as your success grows to have a way to manage the success. The success you will find as the strategic plan is realized will come with additional responsibilities. You will find that getting to the point where you feel successful and maintaining the success both take effort. This is why it is so important to find ways to manage the success you create. Find ways to keep the successes of the past going; this frees up your time to focus on the future success.

Having Passion

Strategic planning is an effective way to accomplish your goals. Accomplishing those visions is much easier when you have a passion for the vision you are trying to achieve. Having a passion is going to give you the commitment level you need to execute the strategic plan. The more you focus on the visions that you have a passion for or are good at, the quicker you will achieve the feeling of success. The more successful you feel around your accomplishments, the quicker you will feel successful and the quicker you will find yourself achieving the objectives you have defined and getting closer to the realization of the vision.

Having passion for something you choose to create a strategic plan for is one of the ways to test for alignment. You could create the perfect strategic plan, but if you do not have a passion or a spark of interest in accomplishing the vision, then the odds for successful completion dwindle. Find the visions in life that you are passionate about, find the vision that you can look back on, and feel proud of the accomplishment. Find the vision that suits you and your unique talents as an individual. That is not to say that you cannot choose a strategic plan that is similar to others and feel the sense of accomplishment. It is to say that you will find it much easier to get up in the morning and work every day to realize your vision.

Involving Others in the Vision

The same holds true for those whom you involve in the strategic plan. The reality of life is that you will undoubtedly have people involved in your Life Strategic Plan. That is a simple fact of life; you most likely do not live your life in a bubble, and those whom you are involved with at work, school, and home will become a part of your vision. You might not involve them in your vision and planning, but their presence, comments, and observations about what you are doing will have an impact on your ability to realize the vision. For this reason you must choose carefully who should be involved in the vision.

The comments and criticism of others will impact your ability to think clearly about the vision and also your execution of the projects. If you believe in a vision and believe in the benefits of realizing the vision, then surround yourself with those who share a similar passion and belief. If you find yourself with those who do not share the passion and believe that you can accomplish the vision, and if the vision is important enough to you, then you must choose between the vision and keeping those around you happy. If the vision is more important than the acquaintances you keep, then consider other acquaintances. At the end of the day when all is said and done, you have a vision of who you want to be. You have a sense of entitlement to your own vision. Don't let others keep you from realizing the vision you hold. Keep those who share the vision and support your effort close.

Share Your Visions

Opportunity plus preparation equals success. With your newly crafted strategic plan in hand, it is important to start thinking about the success you will have. You have spent time creating the strategic plans for your vision, which is the first step. After you have crafted the perfect strategic plan, you will need to be ready to share it with others. While your vision or strategic plan might not require others' participation to meet your vision, for those strategic plans that do, it is important to gain experience sharing the plan, if for nothing more than to get the experience presenting your ideas and getting the feedback so you can update the plan.

Keep the Strategic Plan Handy

In the new digital age, with access to smart devices, intelligent phones, and computers that are getting more and more sophisticated every day, we have a lot of ways of managing our time and what we focus on. You have so many different calendaring options, planners, and sticky notes that you can use to remind you of what needs to be done. The flaw with our calendaring systems is that we don't use them correctly. We put on the calendar what we have to do, not what we want to do. By putting what you have to do, you are letting your vision be set by others. You are following a strategic plan to "the status quo." If you take back the control of the calendar you can affect your vision. Given that a strategic plan can be simple or complex, consider the tools you are going to use to keep the strategic plan at the forefront. A simple strategic plan you could store on a sticky note and place on the dashboard of your car. It doesn't matter what mechanism you use to recall the strategic plan but just that you recall it. The more complex strategic plans will need to have a more formal planning mechanism, but that will come over time. We want to start the thought process first and then focus on how we manage the strategic plan. Look for ways to automate your plan so that you can automatically meet your vision.

Practice the Strategic Plan

THE BEST WAY TO gain experience in building strategic plans is to just start building them. You can build an elaborate strategic plan that defines where your company will be in the next five years or solve something like figuring out what exercise program, if any, you should start. It would be better to start with a simple vision. You are going to start from scratch and build a simple strategic plan that you can use to realize a vision. Recall that our sample strategic plans have seven attributes: vision, goals, strategies, objectives, initiatives, road maps, and projects. You are going to start with the vision and work your way down to your projects. For a simple strategic plan you might not use all the attributes, so use the ones that make sense.

Before you start working on the strategic plan, you need to be in the right frame of mind. You can do this by permitting yourself to be successful. Only you can determine if you can be successful at building a strategic plan. You also want to be working on something you are passionate about. If you are building a strategic plan for something you have zero interest in, it will be much harder than for something you are passionate about. You also have to trust in yourself. You may not see yourself as a strategic thinker, but you are—you make strategic decisions every day. Take the time to build the strategic plan. Learning about a strategic plan without creating one has little value, so commit to building a plan. With a defined strategic plan it is up to you to realize the vision, the blend of strategic decision making that helped you create the strategic plan and the tactical you are already so good at.

- Permit yourself to be successful.
- Find your passion.
- Trust in yourself.
- Build your strategic plan(s).
- Realize your vision.

Vision

Exercise to build a simple strategic plan.

First, define the vision for your strategic plan either in your head or on a sheet of paper and write it down. The vision should be very high level. As you are writing down the vision, think about the idyllic state, what the best outcome for the vision is.

An idyllic state could be something like:

Vision: Increase sales for quarter.
Vision: Get As this semester.
Vision: Have an amazing date night.
Vision: Bake a perfect apple pie.

With the vision defined you want to check for alignment. A helpful tool when thinking about the vision is to answer the whos, whats, whens, wheres, and whys. Who is the vision for? What is it trying to accomplish, and when do I want to accomplish this by? Where does all this take place? Why am I doing this? If you can answer all the questions, you can validate to yourself if this is a good vision to work on.

What is the vision you are thinking of?

Check to make sure:

- The vision is future state and not current state.
- The vision is the ideal outcome.

Goals

Second, create the goals. The goals are the qualitative outcomes that define the vision. A qualitative goal describes the qualities of the vision; you could have goals that describe the quality of the goal that defines the vision. To support the vision of "Increase sales for quarter," we might have a goal of best monthly sales average. For the vision of "Have an amazing date night" we may define a goal of a fantastic dinner. These are qualitative goals. We could go back and prove some of these goals qualitatively, but there most likely won't be any quantitative measurements in the goal.

Vision: Increase sales for quarter.
Goal: Best monthly sales average.

Vision: Get As this semester.
Goal: All As on my tests.

Vision: Have an amazing date night.
Goal: Fantastic dinner.

Vision: Bake a perfect apple pie.
Goal: Great-looking pie.

Alignment check: You always want to check alignment with the vision. Ask yourself if the goals are in alignment with the vision. If necessary, go back and do the who, what, when, where, and why test to see if the goals are all feasible. Above all, do the sanity check to see if the goals are attainable. If you had a goal of highest sales in your industry for the month, you might have a hard time realizing the vision. You want to be realistic with your goals.

- What are the goals that support your vision?

- Your goals should be in alignment with the vision.
- Your goals should be qualitative, *not* quantitative.

Strategies

Third, create your strategies. With a vision and goals that are in alignment, you can start to focus on the strategies to achieve the goals. Also consider what milestones you are looking to achieve. We have qualitative goals defined, but there are milestones we can create to give us an idea if we are on track to meet the goals. If you like to solve problems, the strategy is the place you get to do it. Think about all the ways you could meet the milestone of having the "Best monthly sales average." You could increase sales from existing accounts or hire another sales rep to make more calls. You can fill in a number of other strategies that you could do to meet the goals. Notice that we have not put any numbers next to our goals; we are looking at the macro level to try to determine what the strategies could be.

Vision:	Increase sales for quarter.
Goal:	Best monthly sales average.
Strategy:	Increase sales from existing accounts.
Strategy:	Hire another sales representative.
Vision:	Get As this semester.
Goal:	All As on my tests.
Strategy:	Hire a tutor.
Strategy:	Spend more time studying.

Vision:	Have an amazing date night.
Goal:	Fantastic dinner.
Strategy:	Research best restaurants.
Vision:	Bake a perfect apple pie.
Goal:	Great-looking pie.
Strategy:	Take a cooking class.
Strategy:	Ask baker at local shop for guidance.

- What are some strategies that support the goals you defined earlier?
- Your strategies should be in alignment with the goals.
- Your strategies should be action-oriented.
- Your strategies are the secret sauce to realizing your vision. If you have trouble coming up with the strategies, then research, consult with others, and test the strategy.

Objectives

Fourth, create the objectives. You defined the milestones and strategies you can use to accomplish the goals you created. Now is the time to create the quantitative results to support your strategies.

Vision:	Increase sales for quarter.
Goal:	Best monthly sales average.
Strategy:	Increase sales from existing accounts.

Objective:	Increase sales from existing accounts by 20 percent.
Objective:	Hire one full-time employee to drive sales.
Vision:	Get As this semester.
Goal:	All As on my tests.
Strategy:	Hire a tutor.
Objective:	Hire a Spanish tutor.
Objective:	Hire a math tutor.
Objective:	Spend 50 percent more time studying.
Vision:	Have an amazing date night.
Goal:	Fantastic dinner.
Strategy:	Research the best restaurants.
Objective:	Find three restaurants with four-plus stars.
Objective:	Read at least three reviews online.
Vision:	Bake a perfect apple pie.
Goal:	Great-looking pie.
Strategy:	Take a cooking class.
Strategy:	Ask a professional.
Objective:	Ask the local baker for guidance or tips on the perfect pie.

The objectives are all quantitative; we can measure our success. You will know if you increase sales by "20 percent"; you will know if you "hired one full-time salesperson." Your objectives are measurable; you will know if you are successful or not.

- What are your objectives?
- Objectives are quantitative.
- They should define the strategy milestones.

Initiatives

Define the initiatives: By now you have defined what quantitative objectives you are looking to achieve; you have also defined the milestones by creating strategy statements. The initiatives are the actions you need to do to accomplish the strategy objectives. What are the broad actions you could put in place to help you achieve the strategy milestones?

Take, for instance, the "Increase sales from existing accounts by 20 percent" objective. There are several ways to do this: you could create a marketing campaign or you could offer a reward or loyalty program to customers who spend above a certain limit.

Vision:	Increase sales for quarter.
Goal:	Best monthly sales average.
Strategy:	Increase monthly sales average on new accounts.
Strategy:	Increase sales from existing accounts.

Objective:	Increase sales from existing accounts by 20 percent.
Objective:	Hire one full-time employee to drive sales.
Initiative:	Start a marketing plan.
Initiative:	Loyalty program for spending above a set limit.
Initiative:	Start looking for sales professional.
Initiative:	Take an ad out in the paper.
Vision:	Get As this semester.
Goal:	All As on my tests.
Strategy:	Spend more time studying.
Strategy:	Hire a tutor.
Objective:	Hire a Spanish tutor.
Objective:	Hire a math tutor.
Objective:	Ask friend for references to math tutors.
Objective:	Spend four hours more per week studying.
Initiative:	Start homework right after school.
Initiative:	Etc.

Initiatives are the broad actions that accomplish strategy objectives.
- What are your initiatives?
- Your initiatives should be quantitative.
- Time-sequenced initiatives should be put into road maps, not into initiatives.

Road Maps

Define the road maps. Road maps are time-sequenced initiatives. The strategic plan you are working on could be a road map in other strategic plans, or you might call out to other strategic plans. In your case, just think of the initiatives that are pretty clearly defined; they have a starting point and an ending point.

Vision:	Increase sales for quarter.
Goal:	Best monthly sales average.
Strategy:	Increase monthly sales average on new accounts.
Strategy:	Increase sales from existing accounts.
Objective:	Increase sales from existing accounts by 20 percent.
Objective:	Hire one full-time employee to drive sales.
Initiative:	Start a marketing plan.
Initiative:	Loyalty program for spending above a set limit.
Initiative:	Start looking for sales professional.
Initiative:	Take an ad out in the paper.
Road map:	Marketing road map -> Hire marketing company -> Develop campaign; run campaign -> Measure results.

Road map:	New Hire road map -> Hire another sales representative-> Start looking for a sales professional -> Take an ad out in the paper -> Hire a recruiting firm -> Interview candidates -> Select best qualified.
Vision:	Get As this semester.
Goal:	All As on my tests.
Strategy:	Hire a tutor.
Objective:	Hire a Spanish tutor.
Objective:	Hire a math tutor.
Objective:	Spend four hours more per week studying.
Initiative:	Start homework right after school.
Initiative:	Etc.
Road map:	Join a study club -> Meet twice a week to review homework and prep for tests.

Road maps are time-sequenced initiatives within a strategy.

What are your road maps?

Projects

Projects involve grouping the initiatives to achieve the objectives. The project is the implementation of the initiatives to reach the goals defined by the strategy to realize the vision.

Discover the Secret of the Greats

Vision:	Increase sales for quarter.
Goal:	Best monthly sales average.
Strategy:	Increase monthly sales average on new accounts.
Strategy:	Increase sales from existing accounts.
Objective:	Increase sales from existing accounts by 20 percent.
Objective:	Hire one full-time employee to drive sales.
Initiative:	Start a marketing plan.
Initiative:	Loyalty program for spending above a set limit.
Initiative:	Start looking for sales professional.
Initiative:	Take an ad out in the paper.
Road map:	Marketing road map -> Hire marketing company -> Develop campaign; run campaign -> Measure results.
Road map:	New Hire road map -> Hire another sales representative -> Start looking for a sales professional -> Take an ad out in the paper -> Hire a recruiting firm -> Interview candidates -> Select best qualified.
Projects:	Hire a sales consultant to help develop loyalty program; hire a marketing firm to create a marketing campaign that will increase sales by 20 percent for this month.

What are the projects for your vision?

Conclusion

YOU ARE FOLLOWING A strategic plan whether you want to be or not—the strategic plan for your life is your destiny. The decisions you make on a daily basis all impact your outcome in life. The goals are the life accomplishments that you are so proud of or not so proud of.

For companies, at the macro level, it is the end result for the company. What is the outcome of the company? Did the company succeed? Did it fail? They also have micro goals they are driving toward, such as did we meet our quarterly numbers? Did we meet our yearly goals? Did we add customers this year or lose customers? Strategic plans are helpful to both life and business experiences.

You are using the strategic plan to help you organize your thoughts and become a strategic thinker. Think at the macro level but be able to work on the micro strategy to get you to the end state. Strategic plans can be used throughout your life and business whenever you want to use a strategic-planning tool to help you think strategically about your current state and help define a future state that you can then realize. By building a strategic plan you start at a very high level with a vision and build more and more detail into the plan to a point where you have specific actionable projects you can follow to realize the vision. You are the one who owns the vision of where you want to be in the world. You can realize the vision, but only if getting to that vision is important enough. Then you should start to determine what goals are going to get you to that vision. It is healthy and okay to share your dreams and goals. If you find people who don't support you, then find new friends who do support your goals. Why put yourself at a disadvantage by associating yourself with people who do not share your mind-set, people who aren't results-oriented and are okay with just getting through life? For others, and most likely you, since you have gotten this far, it is important to have that vision defined and to take steps every day to get there.

    The strategic plan is not just a macro tool to help you be successful in your endeavors but is also used at the micro level. The whole is equal to the sum of the parts, or in some cases better than the sum of the parts. The same tenet is true of the strategic plan. Your little accomplishments in life can all be qualified into micro strategic plans. These micro plans are using the same components that you use in the macro but at a smaller scale and over a shorter period of time. Your choices in life affect your final destination. Choose wisely and you will be rewarded; choose incorrectly and you will be set back. Use the tools from the strategic plan to help you make the right decisions.

Strategic-planning skills can be used by everyone in life. You do not have to be an executive of a company; you do not have to be the head of the household to think strategically. If you work for a company in the mail room you can use the same principles to help you accomplish your vision. Think about the vision. First define the who, what, when, where, and why. Are you looking to create a vision for yourself or for the company? With that in mind, you can work on the vision, goals, strategies, objectives, initiatives, road maps, and projects to realize the goal. You could create a tactical strategic plan to solve a challenge in the mail room and then solve another challenge using the process. Get good at the process and you will be elevated to being a strategic thinker in the mail room. You will either be recognized and can move on or you can use your accomplishment to find a job in another company that is looking for strategic thinkers who want to control their destiny or vision for themselves, the department, or the company.

Strategic plans are not just for becoming supersuccessful and dominating in business and our personal lives. Becoming a strategic thinker can help you with your personal life as well. Using the skills you have learned can help you raise your children, do better on your homework study habits, solve a problem, and approach just about anything you can think of solving. You can use the strategic-planning skills to determine who you are going to date. You can determine what the vision is for your love life. Are you looking for a friend? Are you looking for someone to do things with? Do you want someone who is your polar opposite? By creating a strategic plan you can come up with a strategy to help you meet the person who is most like the vision. If you determined what you were looking for, you could feel better about targeting places with potential life partners rather than hoping and wishing someone would come along.

Strategic-planning skills should be used on a daily basis to help you realize your goals. To become a strategic thinker, you will need to think about and work on your skills on a daily basis. This isn't something that you can do once and put away for a year and then come back and review yearly. Making good decisions requires effort; it requires understanding what the macro vision is and making sure that the micro goals you are working on are supporting it. In the future-state vision, you can be in control of your own strategic plan. Thinking daily about what you are trying to accomplish will give you a better chance of achieving your vision.

You are going to need to do periodic reality checks in creating a strategic plan. As you build your strategic plan, you will need to evaluate the projects and initiatives you are currently working on. You will most likely need to do some course correction to help get back on track. This means disengaging from activities that are not in alignment with the vision and starting new initiatives and projects that are better aligned with the vision. This can be very challenging for just about everyone. You might have been in a position where you were accountable for something you got pulled into many years previously. You don't want to do it but are doing it anyway. You continue to do the thing you are doing because you feel that you are expected to do it rather than being something you want to do. There will be tough choices you need to make to realize the visions you have.

Becoming a success will take time; it will take your time to make it happen. It might be time you do not have or do not think you have. Assume that you are married with no degree and four children and you want to get a college education. That is going to take time that you might not think you have. It also is going to take resources that you don't think you have. You can make it happen. You are going to need to start thinking strategically and see how to accomplish the vision you have. Others are in the same position and have found ways to realize the vision. You can, too, but you must set aside the time to focus on your strategic plan, focus on the vision you have, and put a lot of attention and thought into the strategic plans. You will be amazed at how quickly you can become a strategic thinker and start making the decisions to help you get close to your vision.

One of the most important elements of becoming successful is the belief that you can. You will need to build the confidence that this is something you can do. There are going to be people in your life who have no qualms about putting you down or telling you that you are not good enough to do something. There is a much stronger inner voice inside you that shows the naysayers that you can realize your visions and that their negative comments are only fuel to help you work even harder. The best revenge is success. You have the tools in the strategic plan to be successful; now use the tools to achieve the success you deserve.

Realizing the vision is going to take a certain amount of effort. If you have a 90 percent will to be successful in your vision, this is so much more important than talent. You might have a friend who is supertalented, who was put on a pedestal in high school, was perhaps even the valedictorian—but where is that person now? You might know several. Are they as successful now as when they were in high school? They might not be. Their success was the proverbial fifteen minutes of fame. They were successful at school but not successful at strategic thinking. You could be a high school dropout, and if you have a vision and the will to be successful you can be just as successful as the PhD. If you have a vision that you believe in, go for it; give yourself the permission to be successful.

Sharing is caring. In the case of visions, you will, at some point, need to share what your vision is with the rest of the world. You should share your vision wisely. There are many people who have all the will to be successful and will take any idea and use it for their own. When you are creating a vision, only share the vision with people you trust. You only want to share the pieces of the vision with people who can add value. For many visions you can share the whole strategic plan, but if you have a vision that is something you want to patent or a business idea, be careful how much information you share. The first and most obvious reason is that they could copy the idea. The second and most important reason is that they could say something that keeps you from pursuing the vision. That is why it is so important to look for like-minded strategic thinkers whom you can trust.

Your vision must be built by you and only you. You cannot inherit a vision or take one from the guidance counselor at school. The vision you create for yourself should reflect your personality, your tastes, and who you are deep within. Take the comments and advice of others as just that. A comment or advice is not an edict, and you should feel empowered to filter what they say. Your vision and strategic plan are owned by you and only you. You can create a vision that is out of this world, full of delusions of grandeur.

You have permission to be successful; you can achieve great success by being successful at what you do. True success is not only measured in wealth and power but in having the feeling that you have accomplished your vision and your goals. Those who have the power to think strategically, like the greats, have the ability to make the strategic decisions that lead to their success and the ability to continue to make great decisions.

Good luck realizing your visions!!!

Works Cited

Friesner, T. (2011, October 23). *History of SWOT Analysis.* Retrieved October 23, 2011, from marketingteacher.com: http://marketingteacher.com/swot/history-of-swot.html.

McNamara, C. (2011, October 23). *All About Strategic Planning.* Retrieved October 23, 2011, from Management Help: http://managementhelp.org/strategicplanning/.

Scott, J. (2009, October 1). *Road-Mapping: An Essential EA Skill.* Retrieved October 3, 2011, from techtarget.com: http://searchsoa.techtarget.com/feature/Road-Mapping-An-Essential-EA-Skill.

The J. Paul Getty Trust. (2011, November 1). Retrieved November 1, 2011, from http://www.getty.edu: http://www.getty.edu/about/trust.html.

www.ingramcontent.com/pod-product-compliance
Lightning Source LLC
Chambersburg PA
CBHW030930180526
45163CB00002B/517